GREAT CHRISTMAS IDEAS

GREAT CHRISTMAS IDEAS

ALICE CHAPIN

TYNDALE HOUSE PUBLISHERS, INC., WHEATON, ILLINOIS

Front cover illustration copyright © 1992 by Nathan Greene. Front cover photography
copyright © 1992 by Robert McKendrick. Interior illustrations copyright © 1992 by Karen
Larson.

Scripture quotations are taken from *The Living Bible,* copyright © 1971 owned by
assignment by KNT Charitable Trust. All rights reserved.

Library of Congress Cataloging-in-Publication Data

Chapin, Alice Zillman.
    Great Christmas ideas / Alice Chapin.
       p.   cm.
    ISBN 0-8423-1056-8
    1. Christmas—United States.   2. United States—Religious life and
customs.   3. United States—Social life and customs.   I. Title.
GT4986.A1C455   1992
394.2'68282—dc20   92-7747

Printed in Mexico

99 98 97 96 95 94 93 92
9   8   7   6   5   4   3   2

CONTENTS

FOREWORD

Are you yearning to do Christmas better? Are you looking for alternative celebrations that will mean more? Do you want your activities to release the real spirit of this best-loved holiday that so often seems to go sour with commercialism? Well, you're not alone. "No more plastic Christmas!" seems to be a goal for many people—but few seem to know how to find the *real* Christmas. That is why I wrote this book.

Great Christmas Ideas is loaded with hundreds of ideas for families and friends, no matter what their makeup, to celebrate Advent, Christmas, and New Year's in a better way. Many suggestions are religious in nature; they serve as reminders of what the season is about and whose birthday we celebrate at Christmas. These ideas will lend a hand to keep the spiritual heart in the holidays. Other ideas are designed to help folks rediscover the blessedness of reaching out to others, of giving themselves away to lighten someone else's load. Some ideas are simply wonderful "togetherness" formulas, designed to help family and friends enjoy and appreciate one another more. After all, loving each other is what Christmas is all about.

The section titled "Coping with Christmas" features unique and practical helps for many things, including handling the hurry and chaos of the season; overcoming the "holiday blues"; dealing with budget-busting shopping lists; coping with excited, whiny, or greedy youngsters; and discovering ways to be content and find enjoyment, even if you are spending the holidays alone.

Perhaps your family is looking for new ways and means to give hearty affirmation to the Christ of Christmas. Or, though you may have never prayed together before or are not regular churchgoers, you desire change—more depth, more closeness. My hope is that all of the ideas in this book, collected from every imaginable source, will help families just like yours—families that are looking to take their celebrations beyond tinsel and glitter—to rediscover the true joy of Christmas.

So, go ahead. Choose a few ideas and start making room in your life for the *real* Christmas. You will soon find that these celebrations are the things of which traditions are made!

Alice Chapin
Newnan, Georgia

ONE

Keeping the Spiritual Heart in Christmas

Simple religious celebrations that
will warm the heart of any family

The occasion of Christmas is not the birth of Jesus. The occasion of Christmas is the birth of Jesus! We do more than celebrate a historical episode; we honor a[n] . . . identifiable person. (*Alive Now* magazine)

Because we believe, we celebrate and rejoice. Christmas ought to be very, very merry. But when we celebrate lightly, without reflecting much of the deeper meaning of the season, we are cheating both ourselves and others. Each Yule season brings new opportunities for spiritual renewal and for passing on precious parts of our faith to new generations. For their sakes, and for Jesus' sake, we dare not allow Christmas to become distorted until it is little more than a time of empty festivities. We must make it vibrantly clear that we know exactly what we are doing. We must not confuse celebration with entertainment. We must learn creative ways to tell often the Good News about God in our midst during the Yule season. Then Christmas will take on new meaning and bring personal fulfillment for everyone involved.

Getting Started

It's a question we face every year: How do you plan a meaningful family celebration of God coming to earth when children's minds are distracted by an avalanche of television ads (all promoting enticing high-tech toys), department stores (loaded with teen jeans that cost half of a week's wages), and Santas (peeping appealingly out of every downtown window)? An even more difficult question many face is how to change things for the better when your family insists on doing things the way they've always done them.

Well, here's the answer: You make up your mind to do it, then you do it! You recognize that even children sometimes feel hollow and confused in the aftermath of candy canes, littered gift wrappings, and strewn piles of toys. Though you may find it hard to believe, children sense when there has not been a satisfying inner celebration honoring the Creator of Christmas. Many people with whom I have talked admitted to feeling an uneasiness, even a vacuum, about continuing with some "traditional" Christmas celebrations that reflected little of Christ. Several wondered how those "traditions" ever got started!

If you are ready to reclaim your Christmas, if you want to take charge and begin to reflect the true wonder and meaning of the season, here is how you can begin. Gather the family together after Thanksgiving dinner or some other evening in November (be sure to set this up several weeks ahead so everybody can keep the time free) to read the following C. S. Lewis essay, "Xmas and Christmas" (which is an account of a visit to the imaginary land of Niatirb). After the reading, view one of these filmstrips: The Celebration Revolution of Alexander Scrooge, ($5) or Have Yourself a Merry Little Christmas ($4; $25 in video). (You can attain these filmstrips, along with their respective leader's guides, from Alternatives, P.O. Box 429, 5263 Bouldercrest Road, Ellenwood, GA 30049.) If you cannot find the filmstrips, or if you simply prefer not to use one, use the discussion questions listed after the essay on page 6. You should find yourselves in a lively discussion about how the coming of the King of kings is celebrated, often without a great deal of attention to or reverence for him. You probably will find, as many others have before you, that these materials will be instrumental in leading you and your family to ask how you all can honor God more in your celebrations.

"Xmas and Christmas"
by C.S. Lewis

In the middle of winter when fogs and rains most abound the [people of Niatirb] have a great festival which they call Exmas, and for fifty days they prepare for it in the fashion I shall describe. First of all, every citizen is obliged to send to each of his friends and relations a square piece of hard paper stamped with a picture, which in their speech is called an Exmas-card. But the pictures represent birds sitting on branches, or trees with a dark green prickly leaf, or else men in such garments as the Niatirbians believe that their ancestors wore two hundred years ago riding in coaches such as their ancestors used, or houses with snow on their roofs. And because all men must send these cards the market-place is filled with the crowd of those buying them, so that there is great labour and weariness.

But having bought as many as they suppose to be sufficient, they return to their houses and find there the cards from any to whom they also have sent cards, they throw them away and give thanks to the gods that this labour at least is over for another year. But when they find cards from any to whom thy have not sent, then they beat their breasts and wail and utter curses against the sender and, having sufficiently lamented their misfortune, they put on their boots again and go out into the fog and rain and buy a card for him also. And let this account suffice about Exmas-cards.

They also send gifts to one another, suffering the same things about the gifts as about the cards, or even worse. For every citizen has to guess the value of the gift which every

friend will send to him so that he may send one of equal value, whether he can afford it or not. And they buy as gifts for one another such things as no man ever bought for himself. For the sellers, understanding the custom, put forth all kinds of trumpery, and whatever, being useless and ridiculous, to sell as an Exmas gift. And though the Niatirbians profess themselves to lack sufficient necessary things, such as metal, leather, wood and paper, yet an incredible quantity of these things is wasted every year, being made into the gifts.

And the sellers of gifts no less than the purchasers become pale and weary, because of the crowds and the fog, so that any man who came into a Niatirbian city at this season would think some great public calamity had fallen on Niatirb. This fifty days of preparation is called in their barbarian speech the Exmas Rush.

But when the day of festival comes, then most of the citizens, being exhausted with the Rush, lie in bed till noon. But in the evening they eat five times as much supper as on other days and, crowning themselves with crowns of paper, they become intoxicated. And on the day after Exmas they are very grave, being internally disordered by the supper and the drinking and reckoning how much they have spent on gifts and on the wine."*

Discussion Questions

1. How much money do you think Americans spend on retail buying at Christmas? (More than $25 billion, according to one source!) Discuss how much of this money goes to

*Extract from "Xmas and Christmas" from God in the Dock, copyright © 1970 by C.S. Lewis Pte Ltd, reproduced by permission of Curtis Brown Ltd., London.

self-indulgence even while there are indigent, hungry, needy, homeless folks right in your own community.

2. Has our family gotten caught up too much in the "Xmas" rush? In what ways? How can we make Christmas happy without buying things?

3. In what ways is our Christmas celebration most satisfying to you? Exasperating? What was the best Christmas you can remember? What made it mean so much to you?

4. What are the best and most appropriate ways our family celebrates Christmas? What are some of the worst ways you have heard or seen?

5. What helps you remember Christ during this season? Do you think our family could celebrate the religious part of the holiday more? Name some things you would like to do to center our celebration more around Christ and the real meaning of Christmas.

7. Why do you think we give gifts? Why do we give money to charities? How can we as a family follow Christ's command at Christmas to show love to others? Is loving others appropriate to the season? Why?

8. Shall we purchase a book of Advent activities to help us spend time together looking forward to the birthday of the King of kings? Who will order the book (ask in Christian bookstores)? Which night of the week shall we celebrate? Do you think that we can go ahead even if others do not?

■ Alternative Idea: Request that your church conduct an Alternative Christmas workshop using materials available from Alternatives, P.O. Box 429, 5263 Bouldercrest Road, Ellenwood, GA 30049.

After you've had your family discussion, you will be ready to review the following pages to see what other families have done to express their faith. Possibly yours will agree to try a few of these ideas. Whatever you do, go slowly. Change can be difficult. Some suggestions may be quite different or more deeply spiritual than your family's traditional observances. They may even be out of step with what your more worldly friends do to celebrate. The reluctance you encounter to try new things may seem like sheer stubbornness, but often that's not what it is at all. It may come from the awkwardness people sometimes feel about religious celebrations. If so, chances are good that people's reactions involve strong emotions and unfamiliar feelings. Be aware of this and the ways such emotions could work against—or for—your efforts. Maybe seeing loved ones holding hands around a bountiful holiday dinner table while singing carols together or praying aloud for great Aunt Ella's recovery from a stroke will bring out the handkerchiefs.

It is never too late to celebrate with more integrity, to make room for the real Christmas. Do not be limited by this list of ideas. Let it lead you to create other holiday activities that will be just right for you and your friends and family.

Christmas at the Church

Often when the holiday season arrives, some folks seem to gravitate toward the church where Christmas chimes peal out over the city. And why not? Jesus is at the very heart of the holiday. Dr. Seuss's "How the Grinch Stole Christmas" and Charlie Brown's television holiday antics seem to fade into unimportance when compared to the symbolism and pageantry of Midnight Mass or to the glorious hallelujahs of massive church choirs accompanied by magnificent orchestras.

Even in a small church you can sense the sincerity and closeness of those who are gathered for Christmas Eve prayers and praises. Church candlelight services create a mellow, spiritual mood. Young and old alike participate with delight in the bright excitement of passing the lights on to others. Singing familiar hymns in the friendly glow can help put Christ back in Christmas and make it seem that all truly is well with the soul.

Even if you are not a "religious" person, you may find that you will have a merrier and more meaningful Christmas if you join in several local church activities during the holidays. Most churches have special programs that will touch your heart. Keep your eyes open for announcements of Bible film presentations, music concerts, "live" nativity scenes, even craft hours when folks come together to make unique Advent calendars or Chrismon decorations. (Never heard of a Chrismon decoration? Turn to page 30 to discover how much fun they can be!) Rest assured, whatever church activity or program you attend, you will be welcome!

Bonus Idea 1: Attend at least one Sunday school Christmas program. It is not Christmas until you have heard lively or shy or delightfully reluctant little children, scrubbed and brushed

and dressed in Sunday best, joyously sing "Away in a Manger" at the top of their voices or proudly recite (or not) assigned poems and Scriptures. Small girls dressed as pristine angels or little boy shepherds performing (or not) holiday skits both serious and hilarious, will make anybody's Christmas seem warm and real. And, if there are good children (and adults) in the audience, Santa Sunday School Superintendent just may make an appearance and, with a wink of his eye and a twist of his head, hand out candy boxes. It is truly satisfying, for children and adults alike, to connect church activities with the warmth and fun of good friendships.

Bonus Idea 2: Take the children for a visit to your church's sanctuary on a day when no one else is there. Read the Bethlehem story to them from the Bible on the pulpit, then talk together about the meaning of the church icons (images) and symbols.

Bonus Idea 3: Call any church's office or watch newspapers to find a scheduled time for caroling. Take the children along and join freely in activities afterward. Caroling can be inspiring and fun even without snow. If the weather is warm or rainy, ask folks to carry along big red umbrellas with crocheted snowflakes hung on strings from the edges to remind yourselves and others that Christmas is coming anyway. Or staple lacy paper doily snowflakes to your clothing or hats. Curious and appreciative folks will likely smile a little as they poke their heads out of houses and apartments to view your unusual caroling choir—they may even join in the singing.

Bonus Idea 4: For the month of December, visit morning and evening Sunday services of several different denominations. Church folks usually welcome strangers heartily. This may prove to be the best part of the holidays, as you are reminded that the family of God extends outside your own church and circle of friends. (Someone who is living alone or feeling lonesome might find this activity particularly satisfying. Why not invite them along?)

Bonus Idea 5: Maybe your family would enjoy joining in a Jewish Hanukkah celebration at a nearby synagogue. If you decide to do this, call ahead for permission. Then highlight the visit with a home discussion afterward over pizza. Perhaps you could read Hanukkah stories and talk over appropriate symbols to better understand Jewish celebrations as they relate to twentieth-century Christianity.

At Home with Christ

Sure, the kids may (or may not!) moan and groan when they are pulled away from the exciting holiday hustle and bustle for devotions. But, when looking back, most of us probably will wish that we had spent more time exploring our beliefs and traditions together as a family.

Try to plan a fifteen- to twenty-minute home worship service for your family. Ask Dad (or someone else who is willing) to be the coordinator. Make it easy by requesting that everybody bring along some activity to praise God, maybe an instrument for playing a solo, a prayer to read aloud, or simply a request for a much-loved carol. Light candles and include litany and Scripture reading. If you feel uneasy conducting your family fellow-

ship time, take advantage of the marvel of electronics to let someone else lead. Look in Christian bookstores for family devotional cassettes or for inspirational videos to rent. Perhaps you could borrow a flannelboard, filmstrips, or other visuals from the Sunday school library. (Be sure to view borrowed materials before using them, especially if there are invited guests. After all, the whole aim is to make home worship an uplifting time. Poor materials, or those that do not reflect your beliefs, can ruin everything.)

Bonus Idea 1: Make a big deal of setting aside a time for family Bible reading every day in December, maybe right after supper or breakfast. The Bible is one of the most trusted tools Christ uses to enter our lives, and Christmas seems just the right time to seek him in Scripture. Have everybody who can read locate each day's passage and follow along in their own Bibles. You may even want to ask for volunteers to read verses aloud.

You can make sure preschoolers don't feel left out by giving them a beautiful bookmark to mark the correct passage. Then they, too, will be able to open their very own Bible to the day's Scripture. Older children can follow along with a finger for the little ones, pointing to words as they are read aloud.

Suggested Bible readings:
November 30—Isaiah 42:1-9
December 1—Psalm 89:1-29
December 2—Isaiah 55
December 3—Isaiah 35
December 4—Luke 1:26-38
December 5—John 1:1-10

December 6—John 1:11-18
December 7—Micah 5:2
December 8—Malachi 3:1-4
December 9—Matthew 1:18-25
December 10—Mark 1:1-13
December 11—Isaiah 40:1-11
December 12—Isaiah 52:1-6
December 13—Isaiah 9:2-7
December 14—Luke 1:5-25
December 15—Luke 2:8-20
December 16—Luke 1:39-56
December 17—Jeremiah 33:7-16
December 18—Luke 1:57-80
December 19—Isaiah 61
December 20—Revelation 21:1-7
December 21—Matthew 2:1-12
December 22—Revelation 1:10-18

Bonus Idea 2: Set up an easy daily spiritual activity chart for your family to use, beginning four weeks prior to Christmas. Include readings and activities that will help focus your attention on the real reason for the season.

Choose a special theme for each week. Some options would be Creativity, Sharing the Good News, Being Generous, Caring about Others, Showing God You Love Him, The Magic of Babies, etc.

Following are some suggested activities for each of these topics. (You should plan on doing one activity per day.) Pick and choose those that you think your family would enjoy most, and think up others, too.

Activities for a week on Creativity.

1. Make decorations (garlands of cranberries and popcorn, paper snowflakes, Scriptures written on ball ornaments, etc.) and symbolic tree ornaments (star, cross, manger, lamb).

2. Read the Christmas story together from Luke 2:1-20. Have everyone draw pictures of different scenes from the story on a long piece of shelf paper. Or try retelling the story in modern-day terms.

3. Make creative gifts, such as chore or hug coupons; a promise that someone else can run the TV remote control or sit in the "good" chair; homemade tickets for a trip someplace special (the zoo, a concert, an art museum, etc.); activity kits such as a counted cross-stitch kit, tackle box filled with lures and hooks, or a tool box with unique tools; subscriptions to magazines or coupons to video stores; and so on.

4. Decide how you can make Christmas music a creative part of your celebration. Let each member choose a favorite album to play; write new lyrics to familiar carols; have a family sing-along around a piano or with someone accompanying on a guitar; have a family music recital or a time of reading about the background of carols; pick out Scripture verses about music and make posters with those verses on them; have a music-making contest where everyone has to make an instrument out of a household item (i.e., glasses filled with water, spoons, rubber bands, etc.).

5. Condense a favorite Christmas book or story into a one- or two-act play. Have the whole family, even pets, take part in acting out your play.

6. Choose a Christmas color (green, gold, red, white) and make one day Red Day or Green Day. Fix meals where everything must be that color, either naturally or with the help of food coloring. Wear clothes in the appropriate color, and play I Spy to see how many Christmas items and/or decorations of that color your family can spot.

Activities for a week on Caring about Others.

1. Discuss some ways your family can help someone who might be feeling lonely to feel better. Do you know someone who is far away from home this holiday? Is there a single person or someone who is alone for the first time this Christmas who you can invite over for dinner? Is there some special gift of time or talents that you can share with someone to brighten the holidays?

2. Fix up a "Take-Out" party to share with someone who is homebound. Put hot chocolate mix, cookies, napkins, cups, a book, a game, a video, etc. into a creative package (baskets work well for this). Then take the party to the person's home and spend the evening enjoying it with him or her.

3. Ask each child to select and wrap a good used toy as a gift given in Jesus' name, then donate it to a mission or children's home.

4. Talk about our responsibility to care for animals. Discuss the things you do to take care of any pets you may have.

Can you do something special for the animals outside your home? How about decorating an outside tree with goodies for the birds (hang seed balls on branches; string cranberries, popcorn, raisins, or peanuts on heavy thread and drape on branches; hang pinecones spread with peanut butter and rolled in birdseed). Cut an orange in half, then peel carefully to keep the rind intact. Next, hang half orange rinds filled with suet, sunflower seeds, and bread crumbs on trees or railings.

5. Put a jigsaw puzzle out on a table, then invite some people over to help you put it together. Serve hot chocolate and doughnuts or cookies.

6. Have your family take ten minutes to find as many Scriptures as they can that talk about caring for others. Read Charles Dickens's *A Christmas Carol.* Discuss ways you can share the Christmas spirit by anonymous gifts (food, toys, books, furniture, clothing, etc.). Consider giving the gift of your time to someone.

7. Do something unexpected for a neighbor. For example, shovel their walks, bring them a tray of homemade Christmas goodies, walk their dog, offer your services to help get the house cleaned and ready for Christmas visitors, etc.

Activities for a week on Sharing the Good News.
1. Discuss how you can witness to others through your preparation and decorations this year. Decide to be kind and encouraging to clerks in stores. Give only homemade gifts this year and donate the money you save. Write your post-

man a note of thanks for all his hard work and for taking part in helping you stay in contact with those you love.

2. Make Christmas cookies to give to neighbors.

3. Ask someone who may be lonely to go out with your family to look at decorations and window displays. Judge the displays to decide which one best communicates the true meaning of Christmas. Sing carols as you go from house to house.

4. Designate one meal as the Good News Meal. Only good news may be shared.

5. Read Luke 2:13-14, then make a "Share the Good News Paper." Have everyone contribute articles that share the joy of Jesus' coming. Make up imitation ads and articles, such as an ad for hay to fill the mangers or feed for the animals in the stable; a birth announcement for Christ; an interview with the wise men or with King Herod; a report on the concert given by Hark and Herald's Angels in the sheep pasture near Bethlehem, etc.

6. Memorize Luke 2:1-14, with each member doing a separate part. Recite it for guests at Christmas.

Bonus Idea 3: Conduct your own Christmas Eve worship service. Many people have grown up going to midnight services on Christmas Eve. It is a tradition they enjoy and continue as adults. However, when small children come into the picture, the tradition can border on trauma. Keeping children awake for the service, getting them dressed, keeping them quiet during the ser-

vice—all of this can reduce or even eliminate the pleasure for parents. And when children are tired and cranky the next day, it can hinder a family's enjoyment of Christmas as well.

Instead of going to a church service, consider having a service in your home. Decide as a family what you would like to include in your service, what time to start and finish, and what you will wear. You may want to dress up, or you may want to have everyone get into their pajamas so that they can head for bed as soon as the service is over.

Work on the service together. Here are some possible ideas: share favorite hymns or readings, choose appropriate Scripture, make a drawing of something you are thankful for, etc. Everyone must come up with something to share. Also, agree together on a special Christmas story to read (in addition to the Christmas story in Luke). Some possibilities include shortened versions of Dickens's *The Christmas Carol,* O. Henry's *The Gift of the Magi,* or portions of the delightful book *The Best Christmas Pageant Ever.*

On Christmas Eve, at the chosen starting time, light candles around the room. Have everyone file in singing a favorite Christmas carol. Each person could carry something to set beneath the Christmas tree, such as a figure from the family nativity scene or a wrapped gift for the baby Jesus. Then have everyone sit around in a close circle, and ask someone to read the Christmas story from the Bible. Next, read the other Christmas story you've chosen. After the readings, give family members an opportunity to share what they have prepared—songs, drawings, poems, whatever. Close the service by having each family member say what he or she loves most about another family member. Finally, end the evening with prayer and possibly a Christmas snack.

Family Christmas Retreat

Instead of staying home for the whole Christmas holiday, how about taking a family retreat? Consider running away to Grandma's seashore cottage or renting a place to spend the holidays. Wherever you go, be sure everyone understands that several hours of the getaway will be a meditation time. Here are some good ideas for the meditation:

1. Love letter to Jesus. Ask the family to gather while someone reads from the Bible about Jesus' birth (Luke 1:26-35). Then have someone read about how Jesus gave his life freely on the cross as a gift to each of us (Matthew 27), and about his resurrection (Matthew 28). Finally, read Scriptures describing God's greatness, power, majesty, and compassion. (Some suggestions: Job 38–39; Psalm 104:1-35; 107:23-28; 145:17-21; Jeremiah 32:27; Isaiah 48:12-13; 64:1-4; Romans 11:33-36.)

   After the readings, ask each person to find a place to be alone and reread the Bible verses silently, then to write a heartfelt letter praising God. Adults and teens will need to help early readers. Encourage everyone to express feelings of love, awe, joy, fear, and thankfulness to God. Collect the love letters to Jesus and place them in a box to be shared aloud when the family gathers once again on Christmas Eve, Christmas Day or New Year's.

   By the way, you will probably be surprised at the depth of what's written, especially by teenagers who are willing to cooperate in this shared family meditation.

2. Stocking for Jesus. Have someone who has "crafty" abilities crochet or knit or sew a beautiful stocking for Jesus. Maybe

Aunt Lou could cross-stitch a lovely flower, cross, lamb, crown, anchor, or some other important religious symbol. Then have everyone write on a little card how he or she would like to become a better person and be more like Christ. Seal the cards in envelopes (give each person a different color for later identification) and place them in Christ's stocking. After the holidays, have Mom gather the envelopes and return them to the appropriate people as personal reminders for the months ahead.

3. Personal confession. The selected Scriptures on pages 12 and 13 clearly show why Christ came to Earth. They demonstrate his ability to forgive sin and clear the path to God. One family with older children used index cards to write private notes of confession to Jesus, then burned the cards in the fireplace at the end of the retreat hour. This symbolized their personal forgiveness and cleanness before God through Jesus' sacrifice on the cross.

Whatever you decide to do for your family meditation time, consider this ending (if it fits the pattern of your faith and seems appropriate): Ask if anyone is ready to follow Christ in baptism. If someone expresses the desire to do this, be sure to enroll him or her in an instruction class with your pastor, then schedule a definite time for the sacred rite. What more wonderful event could there be than a child or adult committing him or herself to Christ under the spiritual care and instruction of a loving family?

Baptism Celebration

Nothing could be more appropriate than making a baptism or confirmation part of the Yuletide celebration. Writer Phyllis Shaugnessy notes that most families find it difficult to get everybody together for celebrations once children reach the teen years. Here is how Mom, Dad and five grown Shaugnessy children managed to merge schedules to celebrate the Epiphany feast of the Lord's baptism. Maybe you can use some of Phyllis's ideas to assemble everybody for an upcoming baptism in your family.

A Family Gathering

Now that most of my six children have grown and are living on their own, I find it more important than ever to continue the family gathering we began during their younger years.

So as not to infringe on prime-time social hours, when they are apt to have opportunities to share with their friends, my husband and I chose to have our gatherings on Sunday mornings. We try to meet on or near special days in the liturgical calendar

Our first gathering for the new year was on the Sunday following Epiphany [to celebrate] the feast of the Lord's baptism and the final day of the Christmas season. Our invitation went something like this:

You are invited to share in a family gathering on Sunday, January 13, the feast of the baptism of the Lord. It will begin with the 10:30 Mass in our parish church, followed by a

breakfast at home and a time of memory-sharing. Please bring two things with you: a collage of some of your family memories and your sense of humor. We are looking forward to spending this special morning with you. Love, Mom and Dad.

To prepare for this family celebration, I made a mobile with pictures of each family member's baptism, and hung it on a coat hanger from the light fixture over the dining room table. At each place setting was a name tag with the date of that person's baptism on one side and the gospel story of the baptism of Jesus on the other.

We gathered at the church and found a pew near the front where we could all sit together. Times are few when we are all able to attend church together, and moments such as these become times of real family sustenance.

At home after Mass we had a hearty breakfast of ham and eggs, home fries and sweet rolls, and then we spent an hour or so sharing memories. Each person was given time to explain the collage he or she had created and brought to the gathering. . . .

After each of us had shared our memory-collages we concluded our gathering by reading the story of the baptism of Jesus. We offered words of thanks for our own baptism and prayed for help in living out the life of love we are committed to because of our baptism.

Just before the family scattered to other interests, I handed each of them a note. "You are invited," it began, "to another family gathering . . . on the Sunday before Valentine's Day."*

Home Communion

Communion, sharing the cup and the bread, can bond a group of believers or a family together, giving the Christmas celebration a special feeling of peace and harmony. Consider having an annual shared-cup candlelight communion service at home on Christmas night. Invite relatives and friends to join in, and expect a supernatural oneness in Christ despite different backgrounds, denominations, and ages.

Choose a beautiful oversized pewter or crystal goblet to use exclusively for serving the wine (or grape juice). Perhaps Dad or Grandfather will read the story of the Last Supper from Mark 14:12-25. Ask everyone who attends to take turns reading prayers. Then pass around the cup and a small loaf of homemade bread, having each person partake as it comes around. Close your service with caroling. Afterward, carefully wash the goblet and wrap it in a soft white cloth to be put away until next year.

Or, if you prefer, you could conduct a short Christmas Day communion service for family or guests. Consider asking your pastor for a litany, or, if your faith dictates that a clergyman administer the sacred elements, invite the pastor's family to join yours for this meaningful home celebration.

Bonus Idea: You may be unfamiliar with the ritual of footwashing, but it is a beautiful biblical ceremony demonstrating humility and love for one another. The rite symbolizes how Christ came as a servant, in his life and in his death on the cross, to a desperately needy world. At its best, footwashing is a loving yet simple dramatic experience that can unite all involved. "Such a significant sharing of self with others makes Christmas seem far less selfish," says one man who is a member of a church that reg-

ularly practices this rite. Ask your church's religious education director, pastor, or librarian for help in locating an appropriate ceremony. Or call the nearest Free Will Baptist Church for instructions about this unique celebration.

Bible Christmas Trees

You can use Scripture to make your Christmas tree more meaningful. Consider the following possibilities.

Positive Promise Tree

A mother, trying to add new religious emphasis to her family's celebration, says, "Last Christmas, I took about three dozen uplifting promises from the Bible and typed them on tiny red cards. I punched a hole in each card and threaded a slim ribbon through the hole, then tied the cards to the tree. Starting the second week of Advent, the family gathered each evening and every child chose a card to read aloud (we helped the little ones). We spent time focusing on the promise Scriptures, and each person gave an opinion of what they meant. We all learned from each other and loved the time spent together."

Examples of promise Scriptures (from *The Living Bible*):

"Glory be to God, who by his mighty power at work within us is able to do far more than we would ever dare to ask or even dream of—infinitely beyond our highest prayers, desires, thoughts or hopes" (Ephesians 3:20).

"Now in your strength I can scale any wall, attack any troop. What a God he is! How perfect in every way! All his promises prove true. He is a shield for everyone who hides behind him.

For who is God except our Lord? Who but he is as a rock? He fills me with strength and protects me wherever I go. He gives me the surefootedness of a mountain goat upon the crags. He leads me safely along the top of the cliffs" (Psalm 18:29-33).

"How precious it is, Lord, to realize that you are thinking about me constantly! I can't even count how many times a day your thoughts turn towards me. And when I waken in the morning, you are still thinking of me!" (Psalm 139:17-18).

"'The Lord is my Helper, and I am not afraid of anything that mere man can do to me.' . . . Jesus Christ is the same yesterday, today, and forever" (Hebrews 13:6, 8).

"If we confess our sins to him, he can be depended on to forgive us and to cleanse us from every wrong" (1 John 1:9).

"Even when we are too weak to have any faith left, he remains faithful to us and will help us, for he cannot disown us who are part of himself, and he will always carry out his promises to us" (2 Timothy 2:13).

Other encouraging Scriptures: Deuteronomy 31:8; Isaiah 43:2; Psalm 102:17; Psalm 40:17; Hebrews 4:14-16; Psalm 91:1-12; Ephesians 3:17-19; 1 Peter 5:10-11; Isaiah 46:3-4; Philippians 4:6-7; 1 John 3:1-2.

For other Scripture suggestions to hang on the Positive Promise Tree, see *The Jesus Person Promise Book* by David Wilkerson (Regal Books).

Jesse Prophecy Tree

The mystical and miraculous nature of the Christmas season can be seen in the ways the birth of Christ—and many of the events in his life—were prophesied long before he was born. Use a

marker to draw a big tree stump and roots on a large piece of green poster board. This will symbolize what remained of the Jewish nation after it was defeated and ravaged by wars and enemy armies. (The discouraged people yearned for a Messiah, yet hope that the surviving stump of that nation would grow and rise out of its ruin seemed almost nil. Even so, the nation's roots *did* survive and grow, as witnessed by today's prosperous Israel. Their long-awaited savior turned out to be Jesus, the new sprout from the ancestral root of Jesse. He was the prophesied Messiah, though many did not recognize him. Later, we Christians were grafted into the tree of God's children.)

Let the children cut stars out of white foam (foam meat trays that you've thoroughly washed in bleach and water are fine for this). On one side of each star, pin or glue a tiny card containing an Old Testament prophecy about Jesus. On the other side, pin the New Testament verse that is the fulfillment of that prophecy. Decorate your Jesse Tree with the stars. Every evening during December, family members will each take down a star and read both sides aloud. The verses should be a wonderful affirmation of your faith, as you recall how prophets foretold Jesus' birth, life, and ministry hundreds of times—sometimes three hundred years, sometimes more than a thousand years, before his birth.

As an additional activity, choose a set of prophecy-fulfillment Scriptures for everyone to memorize, one a week, until Christmas Eve. Then recite these verses to each other on Christmas Eve. Everyone will be strengthened by remembering how God planned so long for the coming of his Son and by seeing how faithfully he keeps his promises. Doing these things should also help make it easier to trust in the promises God gives us in his Word.

Below are some examples of Scripture for your Jesse Tree. For more Old Testament prophecies and their New Testament fulfillments, see Josh McDowell's book *Evidence That Demands a Verdict* (Here's Life Publishers).

How Christ's coming would be announced
Prophecy: Isaiah 40:3
Fulfillment: Matthew 3:1-3

Bethlehem named as the town of the Messiah's birth
Prophecy: Micah 5:2
Fulfillment: Matthew 2:1-6; John 7:42

Gall and vinegar given Christ on the cross
Prophecy: Psalm 69:21
Fulfillment: Matthew 27:34, 48

Christ would appear to some riding on a donkey
Prophecy: Zechariah 9:9
Fulfillment: Matthew 21:1-5

The Messiah to be born of a virgin
Prophecy: Isaiah 7:14
Fulfillment: Matthew 1:23

Description of Christ on the cross
Prophecy: Psalm 22:1-4, 6-8, 12-18; Isaiah 53:2-9
Fulfillment: Mark 15:22-39

God's Tree

You can use your tree to let others know what our God is like: All powerful! Loving! Forgiving! Always near! Majestic! Worthy of

praise! Wise! And so much more. Choose from the following verses, as well as from others you know, to make up your family's God Tree, a tree that shows the glorious attributes of God. Many of these verses are so comforting and uplifting that they are worthy of memorization.

"I am the Lord, the God of all mankind; is there anything too hard for me?" (Jeremiah 32:27).

"The eyes of the Lord search back and forth across the whole earth, looking for people whose hearts are perfect toward him, so that he can show his great power in helping them" (2 Chronicles 16:9).

"Prepare to meet your God. . . . You are dealing with the One who formed the mountains, made the winds, and knows your every thought; he turns the morning to darkness and crushes down the mountains underneath his feet: Jehovah, the Lord, the Lord Almighty, is his name" (Amos 4:12-13).

"Who else but God goes back and forth to heaven? Who else holds the wind in his fists, and wraps up the oceans in his cloak? Who but God has created the world? If there is any other, what is his name—and his Son's name—if you know it?" (Proverbs 30:4).

"Lord, through all the generations you have been our home! Before the mountains were created, before the earth was formed, you are God without beginning or end. You speak, and man turns back to dust. A thousand years are but as yesterday to you! They are like a single hour!" (Psalm 90:1-4).

"It was through what his Son did that God cleared a path for everything to come to him—all things in heaven and on earth— for Christ's death on the cross has made peace with God for all by his blood" (Colossians 1:20).

"O Lord, you have examined my heart and know everything about me. You know when I sit or stand. When far away you know my every thought. You chart the path ahead of me, and tell me where to stop and rest. Every moment, you know where I am. You know what I am going to say before I even say it. . . . How precious it is, Lord, to realize that you are thinking about me constantly! I can't even count how many times a day your thoughts turn toward me. And when I waken in the morning, you are still thinking of me!" (Psalm 139:1-4,17-18).

"I pray that Christ will be more and more at home in your hearts, living within you as you trust in him. May your roots go down deep into the soil of God's marvelous love; and may you be able to feel and understand, as all God's children should, how long, how wide, how deep, and how high his love really is; and to experience this love for yourselves, though it is so great that you will never see the end of it or fully know or understand it. And so at last you will be filled up with God himself" (Ephesians 3:17-19).

Other verses about the attributes of God: Joshua 1:9; 2 Chronicles 20:15; Psalm 34:18-19; 86:5; 89:7-13; 145:17-21; Isaiah 40:11-13; 46:3-4; Luke 18:27; Romans 11:33-36; Ephesians 3:20-21; Colossians 1:15-17.

Bonus Idea 1: Make thank-you ornaments on which you can write "Thank you, God, for . . ."

Bonus Idea 2: Make Scripture verse ornaments on which you can write the family's favorite verses.

Bonus Idea 3: Make prayer concern ornaments. Write prayer concerns on cards and attach them to the branches. Then, at the beginning of each day during December, have everybody pull down a prayer card and commit to pray for that request throughout the day. Include prayer requests for individuals, the country, important events (weddings, tests, elections, judicial trials, etc.), worldwide peace, the homeless, and so on. If your family has devotions together each night, you can use the day's cards as a guide for prayer.

Chrismon Tree

Your living room will sparkle when you make your tree a Chrismon Tree. You do this by decorating the tree with dozens of white mini-lights (symbolic of Jesus as the Light of the World) and with glistening gold and white ornaments. These dazzling decorations are almost never available in stores, but don't worry! They are simple to make. Simply cut thin white foam into shapes like stars, crosses, a shepherd's staff, an anchor, or a goblet. Some of the Chrismon shapes have been in existence since the earliest days of Christianity. Others are new explanations of God's never-changing presence in this ever-changing world. See page 34 for Chrismon patterns and their meanings. Some families make up their own symbolic designs to match personally inspired thoughts about God. Finish your ornaments by gluing on a trim of gold braid and gold glitter.

Chrismons were actually the creation of one particular church, the Ascension Lutheran Church in Virginia. Here is their story:

Chrismons were first made for use on our Christmas tree in 1957. Their designs are monograms of and symbols for our Lord Jesus Christ. Because these designs have been used by his followers since biblical times, they are the heritage of all Christians and serve to remind each of us, regardless of denomination, of the One we follow.

All Chrismons are made in combinations of white and gold to symbolize the purity and majesty of the Son of God and the Son of Man. Materials used in their construction are white styrofoam, pearls, gold mesh, sequins, fringe, braids, beads, wires, and so forth. Finished decorations range in height from two to twelve inches. In addition to their use as Christmas ornaments, Chrismons serve as educational and inspirational tools throughout the year.

Since the year after our first Chrismon tree, we've been sending instructions and patterns for making Chrismons to churches, secular groups, and individuals of all denominations. The directions are so complete that men, women, and teenagers, even if they have never seen a Chrismon, have successfully made the ornaments.

Over the years, we've added to and improved the instructions. The present edition, which was completed in 1973, consists of four separate books or series: the *Basic* series presents patterns for monograms and symbols for our Lord and God. The thirty designs in this group are more than enough to decorate any tree. Because certain information in

this series is not repeated in the other books, one must have the *Basic* to understand everything in the other series. *Chrismons for Every Day* is for both beginners and advanced workers. The section on miniatures introduces first-time Chrismon makers to the program with a project that they can easily handle. Another section on workshops gives additional helps and outlines. In addition, this book gives patterns and directions for a dozen single Chrismons and a set of eight designs, The Beatitudes. *Chrismons for Every Day* also presents ideas, patterns, and directions for using Chrismons throughout the year as bookmarks, wedding-cake toppers, pictures, arrangements, mobiles, and wreaths.

The Christian Year (formerly *The Liturgical Year*) series combines varied symbols based on seasons of the Church Year. As a unit, the series provides a focal point for the tree; when made up as individual Chrismons, the thirty designs are used in the same manner as the *Basic* ornaments. Several sets and individual designs make up the sixty-some Chrismons in the *Advanced* series. The popular Parable Balls in this series are easy to make. There is no duplication of the designs in any of the series. Each book of instructions contains complete directions and patterns for making Chrismons in that series. Also included are interpretations for every symbol; a worship program (except in the *Every Day*) to explain the meaning of Chrismons in that series; photographs, most at least one-third actual size of the ornaments in that group; sources of materials for making Chrismons; and additional information on how to use and make the series.

With each complete order for the instructions (*Basic, Every Day, Christian Year,* and *Advanced*) we include a free copy of

another book, *Chrismons.* This latter book contains condensed interpretations for most of the ornaments on our church's tree. A full-color photograph of our tree is on the cover while drawings and photographs of some of the Chrismons illustrate the explanations. This book may be purchased separately.

Of course, purchase of the instructions (or possession of the Copyright Release) does not entitle anyone to make Chrismons for sale. We never give this permission.

During the 25th anniversary year of the Chrismon tree at Ascension, a 170-page history of the program, *Chrismons: The First 25 Years,* was published. The book, by Frances Kipps Spencer, originator of the Chrismons, describes the conception and development of the Chrismon program at Ascension, across the nation, and around the world. In addition, it includes illustrations and photographs of Chrismons, Chrismon trees, and people active in various aspects of the Chrismon project worldwide.

While the Chrismons were first intended to be meaningful decorations for our members only, they have become a means of inspiration and instruction for many others as well. Individual congregations build their own Christmas programs and celebrations around their Chrismon trees. In our own church, our tree is lighted every night during Christmas week; we invite our friends and neighbors to gather there with us to hear about our Lord. We invite you, too, to join us at that time as we worship the Christ.

Please address mail to the "Chrismon Ministry" in care of our church (Ascension Lutheran Church, 314 West Main

Chrismon Miniatures

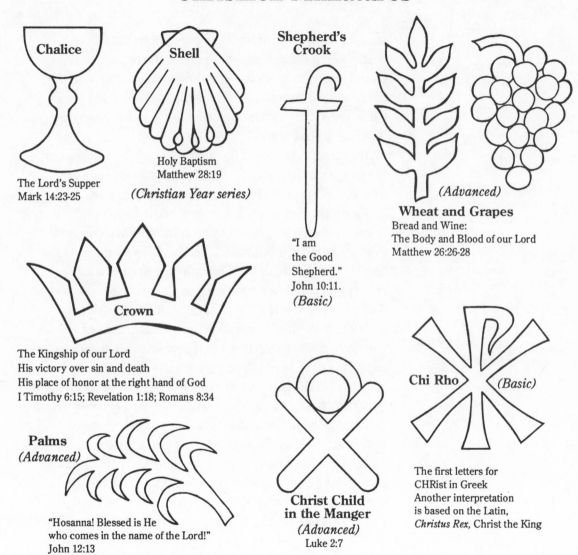

Chalice

The Lord's Supper
Mark 14:23-25

Shell

Holy Baptism
Matthew 28:19

(Christian Year series)

Shepherd's Crook

"I am the Good Shepherd." John 10:11.
(Basic)

(Advanced)

Wheat and Grapes
Bread and Wine:
The Body and Blood of our Lord
Matthew 26:26-28

Crown

The Kingship of our Lord
His victory over sin and death
His place of honor at the right hand of God
I Timothy 6:15; Revelation 1:18; Romans 8:34

Palms
(Advanced)

"Hosanna! Blessed is He
who comes in the name of the Lord!"
John 12:13

Christ Child in the Manger
(Advanced)
Luke 2:7

Chi Rho *(Basic)*

The first letters for
CHRist in Greek
Another interpretation
is based on the Latin,
Christus Rex, Christ the King

Stars from the Christian Year Series:

Five-Point

The Epiphany Star: The Manifestation to the wise men, Matthew 2:2; also Revelation 22:16, "I am . . . the bright morning star"; Numbers 24:17, "A star out of Jacob."

Six-Point

The Creator's Star: Six days of Creation, Genesis 1

Seven-Point

The Holy Spirit Star: The Seven Gifts of the Spirit, Revelation 5:12

Eight-Point

The Holy Baptism Star: Man's regeneration through Holy Baptism, 1 Peter 3:20-21

Street, Danville, Virginia 24541, 804-792-5795). We'll be glad to answer any questions that you may have.

Christmas Story Listening

Choose two days of the week to be used as story nights during December. Then gather the family together on those evenings (8:00 P.M. is a good time) for dessert and stories. In the weeks before, have everybody collect, clip, or copy good Christmas pieces, Scriptures, poems, short stories, brief paragraphs, quotations, and even a few holiday riddles and jokes to spice things up. Place everyone's selections in a big glass bowl decorated with a bright red bow, then set the bowl on the coffee table. During your listening time, have each person draw one item to read aloud, just as families used to do before the days of television. Longer stories can be continued from evening to evening. If you have a fireplace, use it to create a warm and cozy atmosphere. Seat your family in a semi-circle near a brightly burning fire, or set a dozen glowing candles around the room. Serve hot chocolate, a holiday fruit bowl, or some other light holiday snack. Put on tapes or records of quiet Christmas carols as a relaxing backdrop for your time together. You are bound to feel warmed and united by the sharing and by your love for each other. Isn't that what everybody wants at Christmas?

One woman said that some of her happiest remembrances of growing up were the December evenings her family spent around the dining room table. Her dad would read the Christmas story from the Bible, then the family would sit together sharing a special silence, each engrossed in private reading of inspirational books, poems, or stories gathered by her mom from magazines or the public library. This woman noted that

these quiet and warm experiences brought the peace of Christmas to their home.

Christmas Card Listening

All too often we toss aside gorgeous greeting cards after one reading. Sometimes the children in a family never get to see them at all. Enjoying cards and letters as a family is one way to get more out of them, as well as to promote warm feelings of sharing between family members.

Here is a tradition your family may want to begin. Place cards that arrive each day, unopened, in the center of an Advent wreath or in a lovely hand-painted bowl on the coffee table. After dinner every evening, each youngster can choose a card to be read aloud and passed around. Everybody can explain what the message means to him or her. Try to find a picture of the person or persons who sent the card to help younger children understand that cards do not come from the mail person. Encourage older children and adults to tell something pleasant about the sender or to reminisce about good times spent with the individual. Finally, you could write the sender a note, telling him or her something such as, "Our family picked your card out of all our Christmas greetings and we prayed for you today—that God would meet your every need and that your cup would overflow with happiness and Christmas joy." Also, once in a while try to think of something nice to do for the person whose card you have read (i.e., baking a cake, making a phone call, or paying a visit).

Bonus Idea 1: Make addressing Christmas cards into a spiritual exercise. Have older children and adults say a prayer for each person as they copy addresses from the card list. Young-

sters can lick stamps and seal envelopes. Short prayers can be something like, "Father, heal Mindy's allergy" or "Give Steve strength and a quick mind as he learns his new job." You can make petitions silently or aloud with every Christmas card you write. Don't worry if there seems to be a buzz of voices as you all pray for those to whom you are addressing cards. God hears each prayer clearly.

Bonus Idea 2: One recently widowed lady experienced many lonely hours, which was especially difficult during the holidays. She often remembered happier times when she was a little girl growing up in her parents' house. She began to wonder, "Who lives there now? What is the family like? What do the adults do at work? Are there children in my upstairs bedroom?"

One day, she decided to send a note to the occupant at her old address telling that person about herself and how much she loved the old house. In response, she received a truly wonderful gift: a detailed letter telling all about the family and the joy it brought them to live in her former home and to know she held such fond remembrances of the place.

"Next year," she says, "I plan to send the same kind of letter to the current residents of a house my husband and I struggled to build more than thirty years ago. This is the house where we brought three of our four children home from the hospital after their births. I will ask if the tiny weeping willow tree we planted in the front yard is still there and how tall it is now, and about the crazily tilted brick outdoor grill where we enjoyed so many backyard picnics. I am wondering if the living room rug I spent two agonizing days selecting has been replaced and whether the same neighbors live on either side. If the family who lives there

now sends a letter and photo to me as I will ask, I plan to reproduce them as a special gift for my children at Christmas. I think it is a present they will cherish, since each of them has wondered aloud as we talked together about how the old homestead has changed. I can't wait to see how this plan will turn out!"

Bonus Idea 3: Many people express concern about the rising cost of Christmas cards and postage. They especially question mailing cards to those they see all the time. One woman told me, "I have to work a whole day just to pay for sending greeting cards. The money sometimes seems wasted since most of them are promptly thrown in the trash anyway." If you are struggling with this, here's a unique idea that will save time, effort, and money—and help others in the process.

See if a few people from your adult Sunday school class or your organization's officers would take on a simple project. Cover a gigantic piece of plywood with tagboard or butcher paper and ask the resident artist to cut the paper's edges in the shape of a fold-over card. Then print words such as "Everybody's Christmas Greetings Here" on the outside. Set the "card" on an easel or tack it on a wall in the foyer or vestibule of your church, preferably in a place where meetings are held. Then let folks know that they may write their greetings to others in the church on this "community card," and that it can be their one and only card to send to church friends. Worthy wordsmiths will pen greetings and sign their names as they come and go. Busy folks will appreciate being relieved of addressing cards and running to the post office for stamps. Finally, determine a place of financial need in your church or organization, then have each person who signs the card pledge the amount he or she usually spends on sending

cards. After the holidays, in place of the card display put a big bank with a slot or a box with a removable top or bottom where members can place their pledged money.

This may be the very idea your pastor has been looking for to raise money for buying new books for the church library, to restock the food pantry, or to purchase new cribs for the nursery.

Home Art Gallery

"Sometimes our Christmas seems irreverent because we are all so busy going in different directions. We forget to focus as a family on the real meaning of the season." You may be able to identify with the comments of this busy mother. If so, here are some ideas for bringing Christmas home and giving family members a reason to slow down: (1) Hang beautifully colored religious art that is borrowed from your church or public library, or hang prints from December Sunday school resource packets. (2) Stand lovely illustrated books on coffee and end tables, opened to a different page every day. Children will enjoy coming by to see the day's picture. When you see them admiring scenes like the Madonna and the Christ child or visions of the heavenly host, take the opportunity to discuss what each means. Guests in your home will probably appreciate the religious art, too. After all, too many folks do not take time to really enjoy these things at Christmas.

Bonus Idea 1: Is there one thing that you love most about the holiday season? Save Christmas cards or magazine pictures that focus on that thing. Then exhibit these representations. Place them on the mantel, coffee table, or piano top, or hang them with mini-clothespins on a line strung from doorway to

doorway. I have narrowed my selection down to cardinals, angels, or snow scenes. Beginning this December, I plan to add to my collection year after year. Those closest to me already have said they will remember me with appropriate cards.

Another idea is to show nativity scenes one year, the magi another year, then shepherds and sheep the next year. Or you could feature Scripture verses or messages cut from greeting cards. You will probably end up saving every card ever received and beg others to put aside their cards for you so you can make a nice grouping. Collections are fun to do and fun to look at. Family and other holiday guests will be curious about this year's theme and probably head for the display when they first come in the door. Each card is bound to get admired many times over.

Bonus Idea 2: Do you have a big family picture Bible? If so, keep it open on the coffee table during the Yule season. Change to a new page each day, sometimes showing artwork, sometimes highlighting an appropriate Scripture. Young children will enjoy lighting candles on either side as the family gathers in the evening to read Bible verses or for devotionals.

Bonus Idea 3: Make a Christmas frieze or mural for the wall. Spread white shelf paper on the kitchen floor, dividing it into segments with tape. Each family member can fill in a portion of the mural with hand drawings showing events leading up to the birth of the Christ child and the happenings afterward. (Ideas: The early prophets being given messages about Christ's coming, the angel's message to Mary, the donkey ride to Bethlehem, the

inn and innkeeper, the star and shepherds and angels, the flight to Egypt, a contemporary Christmas family celebration scene.)

Bonus Idea 4: Make a wall map of Joseph and Mary's journey from Nazareth to Bethlehem showing the route they may have taken; villages along the way; rivers, lakes, and mountains; and estimated number of miles between places. Knowing about the journey Mary and Joseph took will become much more interesting for those who know where the places are. Children can even clip pictures from magazines or Christmas greeting cards to depict the scene more graphically. If the family enjoys this project, continue with a map showing the flight to Egypt. Read the Bible accounts to get as much information as you can for accuracy.

Bonus Idea 5: Put up a holiday bulletin board by hanging a large piece of corkboard on your kitchen wall. (If you already have a bulletin board, clear off all the old notes, school lunch menus, doctors' appointment cards, and children's school drawings.) Cover the corkboard with big sheets of red construction paper. Cut out letters to form the words "Christmas Is Coming!" to staple at the top, or print the words in large letters. Assign each family member a portion of the board to decorate as skillfully and imaginatively as possible. The only restriction is that at least half of the decorations must reflect the true meaning of the holiday. If your family members seem less than enthusiastic, try this motivation: lay a gaily wrapped gift (use glitzy gold wrapping paper to make it exciting) beside the bulletin board to be awarded to the best decorator. Grandma and Grandpa would probably be honored to be judges when they arrive on Christmas Day.

*Bonus Idea 6:* One year, I tacked up several manger scenes cut from my most elaborate Christmas cards. Then I scrounged around for baby photos of Mom, Dad, and each of our kids and put them on display. At first, everybody poked "kitchy koo" fun about how adorable we all were. But later, when other new and glorious manger scenes were added, attitudes seemed to change. Somebody mentioned during a dinner table conversation how so many families are torn by divorce, death, illness, feuding, or drugs. Suddenly we all knew how much we appreciated having each other and being together. I think that little display helped to remind us that just as the baby Jesus was God's precious gift to the world, each person in our family is a precious gift to the others. One or two tears revealed just how strong the love bonds are, even if that love sometimes seems hidden for days or weeks amidst the turmoil of daily living.

Bonus Idea 7: Try this to capture the joyous colors, feelings, and impressions, the deep peacefulness, and the other wonderful sensations of the Yule season. Make a "Why We Are Glad" wreath to hang on your bulletin board. Cut a big round circle from red or green posterboard or an oversized paper plate, then divide it into six sections. When the family is together, have everybody help write in each space a list of things that are nice to smell, taste, touch, hear, see, or feel at Christmas (some ideas: the scent of pine branches, the beauty of fresh-fallen snow, the mellow glory of candlelight, the delightful ding-dongs of church bells and handbell choirs, the sunny sounds of children's laughter, etc.). Appoint someone to decorate the "glad" wreath in some way, perhaps by stapling a wide, white eyelet ruffle all around or adding a frame. There will be happy talk as everyone remembers

delicious and delightful Yuletide experiences. The enjoyment and talk will continue as you add to the lists of "sensed" things daily, taking note of things that might otherwise be missed amidst hectic schedules or the plastic tackiness of today's commercial Christmas celebrations.

Progressive Nativity Scene

This is a fun way to stir interest in your nativity scene. Start with an empty cradle in the stable and make a big deal of bringing out a few nativity figures each day. Allow small children the joy of arranging and rearranging the pieces as they are added. Start with the crèche and straw, then the animals, Joseph and Mary, the shepherds and sheep, and finally the angels and star. The wise men can be moved a bit closer daily from across the room, arriving well after all the others are in place.

Make comments about each character as it is brought out, reading aloud or explaining what the Bible has to say about each one. For extra interest, make or purchase a few beautiful new figures each year if you can.

Youngsters love the drama of telling and retelling the events this way and will excitedly anticipate the Christmas countdown as the scene nears completion. Perhaps on the evening when the last piece is put in place, the family can sing carols or pray together. Or your family may want to focus on the baby in the manger while an adult leads a short study about the grown-up Jesus and the eventual gift of his life on the cross. When your children are grown, the nativity figures will probably become precious possessions that stir happy memories.

🎁*Bonus Idea 1:* If costly ceramic or carved heirloom stable pieces are too precious for small eager hands, provide youngsters with a less expensive nativity scene just for them. Short on funds? Try painting or pasting figures of the holy family cut from Christmas cards or Sunday school literature onto oversized wooden blocks to help children learn the Christmas story firsthand.

🎁*Bonus Idea 2:* A mother with a newborn baby tied a big red bow around the beloved little newcomer and placed her first beneath the tree on a blanket, then briefly in the bed of straw in an oversized living room manger scene. What a wonderful way to remind her family that their precious new baby was the year's best gift to all of them. By that act, everyone must have gained a better understanding of "the Word made flesh" (see John 1:14). And they probably gained insight into how extraordinary and sacrificial was God's best gift to the world: Jesus, his only Son! Do you have a new baby in your house? Why not try this creative and unusual exercise?

🎁*Bonus Idea 3:* Make a "good deed" nativity scene. Several weeks before Jesus' birthday, set up a stable display with an empty manger (no child or straw). Place a basket filled with straw near the nativity (strips of colored construction paper or Easter grass can be used instead of straw). Tell family members that any time one of them does a worthwhile deed during the Christmas season, that person is to add—unobserved, if possible—a piece of straw to the manger. All deeds should be done secretly, and can include such things as hanging up someone else's jacket, peeling potatoes for Mom so that they are ready to be cooked when she arrives home from work, volunteering to help a younger brother

or sister with homework, etc. Your family is quite likely to feel deep satisfaction when the baby Jesus is laid in his manger, especially since he will be resting on a soft bed that symbolizes your family's love for him as shown in good deeds done for others.

Bonus Idea 4: Somewhere in your community at Christmas there is bound to be a "living" nativity. These nativities have men and women portraying the holy family and shepherds, with real sheep and cows and horses nibbling hay beside the manger containing a real baby. This is a wonderful sight: entire families stand as still as they can, dressed in full costume, usually for one hour shifts, as folks pass by to take a look.

Sure, sometimes it is difficult for all participants, especially the children, to pose quietly. Often the baby or the animals do not behave as we expect, and it is true that Joseph and Mary do tire and droop a bit now and then. Often the weather is wretched—cold, with rain, sleet, or bone-chilling fog. But this only serves to help us realize what it was really like centuries ago for Mary and Joseph. And, sometimes, there is a clear, starry sky and fanciful onlookers can cast a glance upward and pick out what the star of the East might have looked like.

There truly is something enchanting about a real baby in a real manger. Whenever I have viewed such a scene, I confirm to myself, "God's own Son! God come to earth! It is really true, really, really true." In many places, the living nativity has become a tradition, a church's gift to passersby who come from all around to be inspired, uplifted, and to have their faith in Christ as God quietly reaffirmed.

Singing and Playing Christmas

There is always a song in the air at Christmas. The "Hallelujah" chorus, carols played on mighty organs, and chimes that peal from tall church towers all herald joy and peace in our holiday world. Songs help expose the religious part of the Christmas celebration as nothing else can.

You do not have to take music appreciation courses or be musically talented to tune into Christmas. Find carols on the radio or put tapes of Christmas music in the cassette player after dinner or while getting the children ready for bed. Try coaxing would-be music geniuses to play the music themselves on the various instruments. You may think you sound like twelve drummers drumming, but once the initial embarrassment wears off, you may, as our family did, hear an impromptu music group going at it, trying out one carol or another in this corner of the house or that, throughout the entire season.

Better yet, sing familiar hymns and Yule songs together around the piano, allowing each person to select a favorite. Include some contemporary numbers like "White Christmas" or "Little Drummer Boy." Borrow or buy accompanying music tapes featuring magnificent orchestras to make your little amateur group's singing sound a lot more angelic. Most Christian bookstores stock these cassettes.

Why not go together to a Christmas music concert at the local civic center, high school, or music hall? Is there a big city nearby? Urban symphony orchestras usually offer classic Christmas music featuring both traditional, religious, and secular holiday pieces. Most communities have at least one performance of Handel's inspiring *Messiah*. Our four-year-old daughter clapped her hands with excitement as she caught the joyous spirit when the

audience stood up in the traditional way during the "Hallelujah" chorus! Perhaps you can locate a handbell choir performance like the yearly concert in the Huntsville, Alabama, Constitution Hall. Sometimes the ticket cost of events such as these does double duty because money is donated to a worthy cause. One family went home after a hometown concert to a make-your-own sundae party with choices of ice cream, toppings, nuts and candies served with homemade Christmas cookies.

Bonus Idea 1: Here is how Margaret Peale Everett's family provided their own Christmas concert at home.

The Christmas Concert

Three years ago, on December 24th, a special invitation appeared at each of our places at breakfast. It was made of half a piece of construction paper, folded over, with a tiny ribbon poked through holes in one corner. On the front, in bold magic marker, it read:

YOU ARE CORDIALLY INVITED . . .

Our children, Jennifer, age eleven, and Chris, age eight, eagerly flipped theirs open and then looked disappointed. As I opened mine, seeing my husband's familiar handwriting, I read:

. . . to a special candlelight concert of recorded Christmas music, 4:30–5:30 P.M., December 24. R.S.V.P.

"What's this all about?" I asked Paul.

"You'll see."

"But I don't have time to sit for an hour listening to music tonight. We have to eat an early dinner, be at

church at 7:30, and I still have presents to wrap and—"

"You don't have to come," he interrupted. "Just R.S.V.P. 'no.' I will be there and I'd love to have any of you who want to, join me."

The children said 'no' immediately, but I said nothing, deciding to leave it on the back burner of my mind during the day.

At 4:30, frankly, I'd forgotten the invitation. I had just dashed in from a last-minute errand, discovered puddles of melted snow on my newly cleaned kitchen floor and was about to track down the culprit, when I noticed that Paul was lighting all the candles on the first floor of our house.

"What are you doing?"

"It's time for the concert."

Paul flipped on the stereo and the music began. The beautiful sounds of Christmas filled our home. One song after another—from the *Messiah* to "Joy to the World," from choir to solo to instrumental—engulfed me, and I finally stopped my activity and joined Paul in the living room. There, together, as dusk turned to night, we watched the flickering candles send shadows of dancing light all over the room, our bodies and souls quieted by the music proclaiming Christ's birth.

We have now received three such invitations. This past Christmas our daughter, now fourteen, listened from the family room, our son from the kitchen. Each of these rooms was lit only by candlelight. This year my parents visited us. As they opened their invitations, I could "read" their thoughts: *"I can't sit for an hour listening to music."*

However, when 4:30 arrived, they joined us—just to be polite, I'm sure! For one hour we sat still and let the timeless music of Christmas infuse our thoughts and quiet our hearts. And as they left us for the airport two days later, my father said, "I'll never forget that wonderful hour of music. I really felt the spirit of God preparing me to celebrate Christmas."

These days we talk a lot about remembering the spirit of Christmas, but for me, at least, it is still too easy to get all caught up in things to do and places to go. Now I have at least one hour—on December 24th—which brings me back to the heart of Christmas and gives us a chance to meditate on the importance of Christ's birth to us.*

Bonus Idea 2: You will likely find yourself at God's Yule banquets feasting, hugging, laughing, singing. And *dancing?* Yes! Enjoy Christmas any way you can! Use *Dancing Christmas Carols* by Doug Adams, a paperback distributed by Resource Publications, Inc. (160 E. Virginia Street, Suite 290, San Jose, CA 95112), as a source of dignified movement for carolers of all ages. This book presents both simple gestures and sophisticated dance steps. Still wondering whether dancing is an appropriate part of the Christmas celebration? Read Psalms 149:3 and 150:4.

Perhaps we need to be able to act our exuberance in the spirit of Sydney Carter's hymn, "Lord of the Dance," a portion of which says:

> *I danced in the morning when the world was begun,*
> *and I danced in the moon and the stars and the sun,*

*Reprinted with permission from *The Guideposts Family Christmas Book.* Copyright © 1980 by Guideposts Associates, Inc., Carmel, NY 10512.

And I came down from heaven and I danced on the earth,
At Bethlehem I had my birth.

Dance, then, wherever you may be.
I am the Lord of the dance, said he;
And I'll lead you all wherever you may be,
And I'll lead you all in the dance, said he. *

Home Box Office

Don't overlook a readily available resource for family enjoyment during the holidays: your TV! There are holiday specials galore during the Christmas season. Some are wonderful; others can only be considered pitiful. Scan television magazines and choose Christmas programs that reflect the true meaning of the holiday to watch together as a family. Possibly you can select a Christmas music oratorio or a classic drama such as Dickens's *A Christmas Carol* or the biographical film *Jesus.* You may even want to consider an educational offering such as a guided tour of the Holy Land. Why not advertise this family entertainment evening with a few posters placed strategically on bedroom doors? Be sure to have plenty of popcorn, raisins, pretzels, and other snacks for comfy armchair viewing.

Afterward, you can sit around the fireplace and discuss the program. Was it realistic? Did it honor Christ? Did it change your feelings about Jesus or about how the family celebrates Christmas? What was the most inspiring part? Why? Even if the discussion goes nowhere, the togetherness may be worth it.

Secret Angels

In her book, *Prepare Our Hearts,* Muriel Tarr Kurtz says, "If any activity will change the tenor of your home during the Advent season, [Secret Angels] is one of the best! It brings surprises, tears, family fun, and wonder, even if you just watch what is happening to others." Here is the way the Kurtz family does it:

During this season we are to look for and serve the Christ in others. We are to think of others before we think of ourselves, that is, we are "to walk in another's shoes." Our family best implemented this by having Secret Angels for the four weeks of Christmas. As the angel, we tried to look at things the way the person whose name we had drawn would. This included looking at the hardships and perhaps the duties he or she had to do, as well as the experiences which would gladden the heart and delight the spirit. When one chooses an angel, one takes on the responsibility to treat that person in a very special, thoughtful way.

Put each name on a slip of paper and then let each person take a name—not his or her own, of course. It is important to keep the name a secret until a set time when all of you can share whom you have been serving. Some families might choose to reveal the angel at Christmas Eve supper or Christmas morning at the breakfast table. It could be done by putting the angel's name on a slip of paper and tucking it under the plate. Everyone could look at the same time. In our family we hang stockings. The angel stuffs the stocking and reveals his or her name at that time.

The Secret Angels in our family have done many and varied services. We have shined shoes or cleaned a pair of

fed animals when it was not our turn.
ge door opener, opening the garage for
e cherished. Often we have found bed
1d slippers and nightclothes laid out in
all, remember these are acts of service.
by looking at each other and trying to
ould help the other person.
be surprises every day, but there ought
:k's time to assure each family member
that he or she does, indeed, have an angel and that the angel
is watching him or her with interest.*

Birthday Party for Jesus

"How come we give each other gifts at a Christmas party when it
is Jesus' birthday?" asked one confused youngster. "Shouldn't
Jesus get the presents instead?" What a wonderful thought! One
way to bring this idea alive in your family is to have a children's
birthday party for Jesus. A party centered around Christ will turn
kids' thoughts away from themselves and their gift wishes and
allow them to see who is the real star of the Christmas show. It
will help them fit into the season in a unique and fun way, too.

Ask on the invitation that each child bring canned goods, mittens, socks, a prettily wrapped gift marked "girl" or "boy" or an
envelope of money to decorate the tree with dollars. (Be specific
about which kind of gift to bring so that all youngsters bring the
same thing.) Make it clear that their gifts will be donated in the
name of Christ to a charity, nursing home, orphanage, foster
home, hospital, or some other needy organization. Cover a box

*From *Prepare Our Hearts* by Muriel Tarr Kurtz. Copyright © 1986 by The Upper Room,
1908 Grand Avenue, P.O. Box 189, Nashville, TN 37202. Used by permission of the publisher.

with red and green crepe paper, then set it near the front door so children may put their gifts in it as they enter. Paste a large picture of Jesus on the front and hang a poster nearby with the words, "Jesus Is the Reason for the Season." Even young children will understand clearly from this that they give to Jesus himself when giving to others.

One Christmas, Paula Sevier of Birmingham, Alabama, had a party for her children in which the children wrapped their own toys to give to other children. First Paula gathered her children and read them Bible accounts of what Jesus said about love and giving. Then they began wrapping the toys.

The children had brought all sorts of gifts to give away, from toys and books to clothing. When everything was wrapped, they all took the gifts to a fatherless family of sixteen children. Paula made sure her children knew that the reason they were taking these gifts was so Christ could show love through them. What a wonderful way to impress children with the true spirit of giving!

For your Jesus Birthday Party, allow youngsters to have a major role in planning, decorating, delivering invitations, and fixing food. This will give them an opportunity to make holiday events happen rather than being uninvolved onlookers. To get ready, blow up balloons or loop a festive swag of red crepe paper streamers from a chandelier to all four corners of the dining room table.

Here are some good party ideas:

- Bake a birthday cake in a tube pan, decorate it with white frosting and add green frosting leaves here and there so it looks like a wreath. Top it with a bright red bow. Or decorate the top with orange slices, pineapple chunks or some other fruit to symbolize Jesus as the fruit of God's "Messiah prom-

ise," made hundreds of years before he came. Provide candles for the children to light (after the bow is removed) when the children sing happy birthday to Jesus.

■ One mom wrote the names of different virtues Jesus would appreciate, (such as patience, cheerfulness, or honesty) on index cards torn in half. She then rolled the cards up and pushed them at strategic places into the baked cake before frosting it so every child could find one in a slice when the cake was served. Youngsters read their cards aloud and were asked to make it a point to practice that virtue all year.

■ Make a table centerpiece of a small basket filled with straw and containing a tiny doll to represent the infant Jesus.

■ Have your own children make birthday placecards using Yule scenes from old Christmas cards. They can then write guests' names on the placecards.

■ See if your religious bookstore carries small packets of frankincense and myrrh to lay beside a gold-colored article (for example, a necklace or a tiny box wrapped in gold foil) to promote appropriate conversation about articles brought to Jesus by the magi.

Choose two or three of these party activities:

1. Sing simple Christmas carols and fun songs with the children ("Silent Night," "Hark, the Herald Angels Sing," "Frosty the Snowman," "Jingle Bells," etc.).

2. Have an older child read the Christmas story from the Bible or from a picture storybook. Be sure to hold up illustrations for all to see. If there are any "hams" in the group,

provide them with a few impromptu costumes to don at appropriate times. Plaid bathrobes can keep Joseph and the three kings of the Orient toasty warm. The shepherds can watch over their sheep using Grandpa's cane or a yard-stick as a staff. White bedsheets draped over six-year-old cherubs will make them look like real angels should, especially if they are wearing cardboard crowns decorated with gold glitter and satin. A cozy fringed shawl can be draped over the Virgin Mary's shoulders, or she can wear Mom's flowing oriental kimono to conceal the pillow stuffed in her front that makes her really look like a pregnant lady.

When the shepherds enter, break into song with "While Shepherds Watched Their Flocks by Night." When the manger scene is described in the Bible reading, have the kids join you in a quiet rendition of "Away in a Manger." Perhaps some mischievous participant (Dad?) will ham up his part with a bath towel turban and deliberately overplay the somber and gruff innkeeper to provide plenty of giggles. However you portray the story, the tender message of the manger will be clear to all.

3. Plan two or three simple games (such as musical chairs or relay races) just for fun. Why not play pin the tail on Mary and Joseph's donkey?

4. Show a short children's Christmas filmstrip or video (you can probably borrow these from the church or public library).

5. Provide felt, scissors, paste, and other materials and have children make their own Christmas cards. Gift tags can be

fashioned by pasting a pretty design or picture from old greeting cards onto a file card and then clipping it to a two-by-three-inch size with pinking shears. Punch a hole and thread through a ribbon tie. Interesting tree ornaments can be made by allowing the youngsters to paint empty thread spools to look like small drums and looping a silver cord at the top to hang them. Or you could help the kids make a "Christ Is Born!" banner from felt or burlap. Using contrasting colors, cut and glue on felt letters and images such as birds, the sun, flowers, clouds, and people (or use geometric shapes for a more contemporary look). Figures also can be attached with Velcro. When your masterpiece is done, why not draw names to see who takes it home?

6. Hide wrapped candy in easy places for a sweet'n'simple scavenger hunt.

7. If appropriate, distribute children's Good News Comic Books (a package of twenty-five costs about six dollars through Here's Life Publishers, P.O Box 1576, San Bernardino, CA 92424-0001) to introduce children to a personal relationship with Christ. One inner-city mother notes that when the tiny twenty-four-page booklet was read aloud at her children's holiday party, several youngsters said it was the first time they had heard the gospel message. Before trying this, ask yourself if parents would approve (moms and dads on my street loved it when I distributed the little comic books to trick or treaters at Halloween). A book by Darlene Schneider, *Birthday Party for Jesus* (Here's Life Publishers), gives a complete Christmas party plan for sharing the gospel with children ages five to twelve in an

inoffensive, fun way. Included in the book are activities that provide firsthand experiences of God's love.

8. Go to the library for instructions on how to make a children's paper-maché piñata, filled with little sacks of nuts, popcorn, candy, fancy crackers, and other goodies. Hang your piñata, then let children punch it or hit it with a plastic bat until it breaks open and everyone gets to collect and take home the delightful contents. You also could read aloud the history of the piñata to help youngsters see how Christmas is celebrated differently in other places.

9. Make a word game by mixing up the letters of several words from the Bible account of the Christmas story. Ask the children to unscramble each of the words. Perhaps you could have small prizes on hand for the fastest team or person. Or let winners have seconds on dessert! (Word examples: m-a-i-g (magi), g-e-r-m-a-n (manger), d-s-s-h-e-p-h-e-r (shepherds).

Bonus Idea: Why not have an *adult* birthday party for Jesus, with everyone donating a service in Christ's name? One New York man, who was himself a diabetes patient, volunteered to be a driver for Wheels and transport needy folks to and from hospital and doctor appointments twice a week. A woman who had had a mastectomy (and has weathered the uncertainty and setbacks of serious surgery twice) pledged to volunteer time as a counselor in a hospital, helping other women going through the same traumatic experience. A North Carolina contractor pledged to install free door peepholes for the elderly who lived alone in the community. Your adult Birthday Party for Jesus could

well generate a much-needed good deed repository for your neighborhood!

Lighting the Advent Wreath

Anticipation of an event can be as exciting as the occasion itself. Lighting candles on the Advent wreath the four Sundays before Christmas is a visual reminder, especially for children, that Christ, the Light of the World, actually came—and that we need to get ready for his birthday. You and your household can use some of these ideas to make Advent an important part of your celebration, even if you have never done it before.

1. Make an Advent wreath. Purchase a wreath frame made of straw, styrofoam, or wire from any crafts store. Cover the frame with evergreen branches, then push four purple candles or three purple and one pink candle into the wreath. These are, in the order they will be lit, the Prophecy Candle, the Bethlehem Candle, the Shepherd Candle, and the Angel Candle. In the center of the wreath, put one larger white candle, which is the Christ Candle.

2. On each of the four Sundays in December, set a specific time for lighting your Advent wreath. On Christmas Eve, you will light all the candles, including the white candle in the center. When you come to light the candles, have a time of family devotions. Study together the symbolism of each candle. On the first Sunday, you will light the first purple candle, the Prophecy Candle, which represents the prophecies concerning Messiah's birth. The reading for this candle is Malachi 3:1-4.

   On the second Sunday, light the first candle and the sec-

ond candle, which is the Bethlehem Candle. This candle represents the birthplace of Jesus. Micah 5:2 is the Scripture reading for this candle.

On the third Sunday, light the first and second candles, and then the third purple candle (or, if you have one, the pink candle), the Shepherd Candle. This candle represents the joy of the shepherds when they heard about the birth of their Savior. You will find the account of this in Luke 2:8-20.

On the fourth Sunday, light the first three candles, then the fourth candle, the Angel's Candle. This candle represents the part the angels played in Jesus' birth. Read Matthew 1:18-25 and Luke 1:28-38 to see how the angels were involved in this miracle.

On Christmas Eve, light all four purple candles. Then read together the account of Christ's birth in Luke 2:1-20, and light the larger white candle in the center, which is the Christ Candle. As a closing, sing "O Come, All Ye Faithful."

3. Sing Christmas carols together every night at supper and especially on Sundays with your Advent candle lighting.

How Many Days 'til Christmas?: Advent Calendar Ideas

The time from the first day of December until the "Big Day" is longer than forever for small children. Many do not really understand concepts like "Christmas is only twelve days away" or "only two more weeks until Aunt Emma's family arrives." Time passes more quickly for little ones if there is a very special place or way to count days. This is where an Advent calendar can be a big help. Try using an Advent calendar in conjunction with lighting the candles on your Advent wreath, or

with daily devotions, or with some of the other activities
mentioned elsewhere in this chapter. Advent calendars are
especially fun when children can take turns using them each
day.

Here are some ideas for different kinds of Advent calendars.

December Celebrations Calendar

Sometimes, all of our feverishly high hopes for the season
depend on one day. Consequently, we feel disappointed and let
down after all the gifts are opened and our stomachs are full of turkey and dressing. A December celebrations calendar can help
you plan satisfying family activities ahead of Christmas, making
the day itself only one part of the total celebration.

Using a yardstick, mark off squares on a posterboard to make
an oversized replica of a calendar month of December. Paste
Jesus' picture on December 25 because that is his birthday.
Highlight Christmas Eve and New Year's, too. Write an appropriate Bible passage on each day for everybody to read privately
during the month. Select and mark off one day each week for
the family to share some special activity. Perhaps you can agree
to turn off the TV on Thursdays and spend time together reading the Bible and counting blessings. How about naming
Wednesday evenings as "December church nights" or marking
Mondays for early morning family prayers. Now, write in other
activities, such as lighting Advent candles, the church pageant,
a cantata, special worship services, or times when you plan to
watch uplifting television programs. Be sure to look over the
other ideas suggested in this chapter and select a few to write
on your calendar. Let your children choose some activities, too.

They can help "pretty up" the edges of the activities calendar by gluing on pictures clipped from greeting cards, putting on stickers, or drawing a border.

Now for the festivities! When will Grandma and Grandpa arrive? Can the children visit the airport? Which day will be set aside to bake cookies? To visit the mall for shopping? To take a trip to the Christmas tree farm to cut the tree? To gather pinecones, evergreens, and red berries for wreaths? To set out the crèche? To make wish lists? To wrap gifts? What days will you make holiday phone calls to loved ones? (Let the children talk, too!) What days will you help decorate the church? Go caroling? Practice for the Sunday school skit? Prepare guest rooms?

Be sure to leave at least one family outreach time for visiting a nursing home, taking cookies to a shut-in or toys to an orphanage, helping pack Christmas baskets for the needy, or some other activity that involves giving yourselves away. Maybe you would like to set aside a December evening to invite a lonely person for dinner, or mark off several days when each family member will try all day to give sincere compliments to others, to make someone smile, or to complete needed tasks. Everyone will be uplifted by the loving they experience in themselves and from others.

Don't let your calendar end with Christmas Day, either. On days after Christmas, schedule such activities as writing thank-you notes, making New Year's resolutions, taking down the tree, or attending a New Year's Eve watchnight service at church.

A December activities calendar will not only extend the season and make the month more exciting, but it will also add to your

own peace of mind by getting Christmas "things to do" organized on paper. And just watch the kids glow with anticipation about even the simplest events!

🐿️*Bonus Idea:* You can order an inexpensive ready-made Advent calendar with all kinds of great activity suggestions and plenty of room to fill in some of your own from Channing Bete Co., 200 State Road, South Deerfield, MA 01373.

December Prayer Calendar

Focus on one family prayer topic or theme each week. Ask each person to contribute prayer items matching that week's theme. Use a concordance to select coordinating Scripture. Stuck for themes? How about Praise and Thanksgiving Week; God Adoration Week, where you worship God for who he is and for his power, majesty, and love; Repentance and Confession Week; Petition Week, where you ask for God's guidance and mercy in world events and for specific items important in your lives right now.

Remind children to consult the calendar at bedtime or mealtime prayers—and don't forget to let the little ones do a daily countdown of days to Christmas.

Four-Week Prayer Chain

Let each family member participate in linking together twenty-eight colored strips of construction paper, making every seventh one white to denote the passing of a week and making December 25 an exciting red. Children will be delighted to make their chains out of their favorite color, so that Ellie always knows her loop chain is green and Dad's is blue. Have Mom, Dad, or older

children write specific prayer requests inside each link, so that children may remove one link per day during family or private prayer times. Commit as a family to be faithful in prayer concerning the day's topic. You may also want to write something special inside certain loops, such as a surprise family activity inside Wednesday loops (i.e., making Christmas cards for missionaries' children or visiting the Star of Bethlehem show at the local planetarium).

Bonus Idea: Family prayer garland. Gather everybody daily during Advent for "out loud" prayers, then write petitions on paper loops to make one long family chain. Children will love to watch the prayer garland grow longer (and longer!) as the family prays together. This Advent prayer chain can be draped in scallops to decorate the living room and dining area and perhaps wind in and out through the entire house. Only family members will know the special and significant secret about what this ordinary-looking decoration contains.

Thank-You Calendar

Make a calendar of appreciation to God for all he has done, beginning it the day after Thanksgiving. Write thank-you items on each day's square. For example, give thanks on:

Mondays for people who have blessed your life, maybe even ancestors who have passed on a wonderful heritage;

Tuesdays for special portions of Scripture that have helped you (for an extra blessing, read them aloud);

Wednesdays for favorite places and scenes (picture them as you thank God for them);

				NOV. 26	27	28
COOL 29	30	DEC. 1	2	3	4	5
6	RAIN 7	8	9	10	11	12
13	14	15	16	17	18	19
20	21	95° 22	23	24	25	

Weather Calendar

Thursdays for material blessings such as food, appliances, money, automobiles, and a house or apartment to live in;

Fridays for God-given talents, helpful personal traits, and hobbies;

Saturdays for God's attributes that you especially appreciate (i.e., patience, kindness, mercy, guidance, wisdom, etc.);

Sundays for your choice of special blessing.

To add interest for children, have one youngster record each day's weather (cloudy, sunny, rainy, or windy), and let another have the fun of writing in yesterday's high and low temperatures. Keep the calendar to compare next year's weather.

Bonus Idea: Make up a twenty-four-hour prayer chart, marking midnight December 23 to midnight December 24, dividing the chart into half-hour slots. Engage brothers and sisters, cousins, aunts and uncles, and grandparents to pledge that they will pray during assigned half-hour slots. Supply all prayers with a

list of topics so time is utilized to the fullest. One young woman enjoyed the time spent talking with God so much that she accepted double meditation vigils. It is nice to know that there is nonstop prayer going on for loved ones and for yourself.

Cookie Countdown Calendar

Put on your apron, then gather the children and Grandma's best recipe to make and decorate twenty-four luscious Christmas cookies plus one gigantic, extra-special one. Make two of each cookie in case one gets broken. If you can, choose cookie cutters from a chef's specialty shop that have Christmas significance (i.e., a star, a donkey, a wreath, a sheep, an angel). This will provide opportunity for plenty of good talk about the meaning of each symbolic shape. Tell youngsters that the star represents Jesus as God's light to the world; show how the wreath is like the circle of God's love, without end.

Place each cookie in a small plastic bag, slip in a Bible verse, and tie it shut with a four-inch strand of slim red ribbon or yarn. Staple one above the other on a two-yard strip of burlap or sturdy bright red or green grosgrain ribbon. Of course, the biggest and best cookie tops the strip. Let the children take turns removing a bag each day from December 1 to 25, reading the Scripture verse aloud and counting down days left before Jesus' birthday. The super cookie will be big enough for all to share on Christmas Day. (If you don't want to make cookies, fill the goodie bags with candy, nuts, raisins, dried fruit, a mini-toy, or any other lightweight item that will capture a small child's fancy.)

Other Ideas to Help Children Mark Time until Christmas

- Surprise Boxes. One mom fashioned a chimney stack of thirty small identical boxes, about two inches by three inches in size, one atop the other. Every box in the stack contained a mini-surprise such as mints, a trinket, or some other little treat children could enjoy, one each day until Christmas. Or, you could number the little boxes and tie them to a small tree, real or cardboard. If you live near a box factory, go to the office and ask them to save seconds for you.

- Christmas in Other Places. Cut out a thirty-six-inch green posterboard tree and tack it up on a bulletin board or tape it

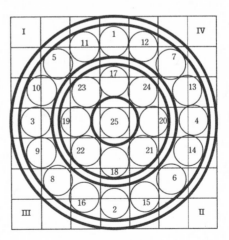

on a wall. Hang any number of small numbered tags on the branches. Let each tag suggest a country that the family can study to learn about its Christmas traditions. Tell younger children how many "tag days" until Christmas, turning tags over in sequence as they are used, one per day. Maybe teens will be willing to do a bit of research, locating library books describing international holiday celebrations. If somebody feels ambitious, how about baking up a dessert or main dish that is part of the tradition of two or three of the countries?

■ The Immanuel. The pattern for a do-it-yourself wheel calendar for Advent is available for $4.50 from Saint Leo League (117 Washington St., Newport, RI 02840). The wheel will help show the importance of the baby Jesus' genealogy. After one family had used this remarkably designed wheel, the parent said, "Gradually, over the weeks of Advent, the sense of epochs began to dawn on the children. They began to understand what 'the Root of Jesse' meant, and that Jesse himself had long roots before him; that Jesus was somehow related to Abraham and Ruth; and that Christmas and Christ's birth are not simply a story, but a factual occurrence; not a remarkable fluke, but an event prepared over the centuries whose worth is so significant we cannot yet understand it."*

*Reprinted with permission from Resource Publications, Inc., 160 E. Virginia St., Suite #290, San Jose, CA 95112.

TWO

Goodwill toward Men

How families just like yours can
find new joy in reaching out to others at Christmas

The Joy of It All

"One rainy evening when our family was caroling to an elderly woman, I sensed a wonder and an uplifting of the spirit that was truly beyond me and my normal reactions. I realized that God was showing me how blessed it is to do for one who can never return the favor in any way. I suddenly felt that I had had a glimpse of heaven, and I cherish that memory. This is not an experience that was only for me. Many have had that kind of experience in their lives. Doing for those who cannot repay is another way God touches us with a happiness, a closeness, a joy that is truly of [him]. Hopefully, you will experience that this season."*

One Christmas morning, I got up before my family. As I sipped coffee in a big rocker beside the tree, I suddenly felt alarmed at the mounds and mounds of lavishly wrapped packages. Furthermore, I wondered how many of the gifts would be wanted or used and how many were just plain junk. It seemed truly irreverent to spend so much money on ourselves to celebrate the birthday of another. I knew that some of the children's most costly presents were war toys or inappropriate playthings. I also knew that giving the kids material gifts has little to do with love. The piles of packages left me with a sick, guilty feeling that cast a gloomy cloud over our holiday celebration. Since that time, I've encountered many people who have experienced this kind of Christmas overkill.

So how do we get out of Yuletide overindulgence? One way is to discuss with your family the idea of giving themselves the "gift of disadvantage" next year so that everyone will be able to pass on some of their blessings to others. To do this, read Luke 4:18-

*From *Prepare Our Hearts* by Muriel Tarr Kurtz, Copyright © 1986 by The Upper Room 1908 Grand Ave., P.O. Box 189, Nashville, TN 37202. Used by permission of the publisher.

19, Matthew 25:31-40, and 1 John 4:7-8 together. Then make a list of caring acts in which family members might get involved as a birthday gift to Christ. Talk about who needs help most and how to get money for projects. Most everyone will agree that while giving tangible things is important, getting personally involved in the lives of the needy has the highest priority. Children probably will accept the challenge eagerly and come up with great ideas, even the little tots. For example, it takes loving hands to help run errands for a shut-in, sew costumes for the children's program at church, deliver food baskets, or collect canned goods and clothing for area food pantries.

After your family discussion, you may find that the kids had been waiting all along for Mom and Dad or other adults to suggest ways to make Christmas less self-centered. Most likely, you all will feel gratified to see Christmas going in a different direction, and you may even come to realize the significance of James Russell Lowell's statement: "Not what we give, but what we share. For the gift without the giver is bare."

Of course, putting ideas such as these into action costs money. How can you finance your family's goodwill activities? Here are some suggestions.

- Are you planning the purchase of some appliance, tool, or household gadget? Explain your new Christmas project to nearby relatives and friends. Then ask if they would like to share in the purchase of your needed item or items. In other words, you will buy one snow blower, fencepost digger, blender, video camera, slide projector, etc. to share, rather than buying one for each household. Then you can put away the money your family saved.

- Accept good used children's clothing from a friend who has older youngsters.

- Children can put away a little allowance money every week in a Christmas "cookie" jar. Other ways they can save are by giving up candy for a month or two, purchasing toys and books at garage sales, and buying items like bicycles and ice skates through newspaper want ads. One mom says, "When our children spend their own savings instead of cash we give them to buy toys for the less fortunate, they look forward to shopping and their attitude seems far less selfish. In the weeks before Christmas, I often hear them excitedly chatting together trying to make up their minds about what they will buy. It adds a whole new element to the holidays."

- Decide to have one simpler meal per week, and place the cash you save in a glass piggy bank so everybody can watch savings grow. One family calculated that having macaroni and cheese with no dessert on Thursdays would save about $3 a week. This resulted in their saving nearly $150 for their Christmas project. The smaller children enjoyed poking coins through the piggy bank's slot, and everybody remarked that "Piggy" made a wonderful door stop.

- Agree to save 75 percent of what would be spent on buying gifts for each other and for an elaborate Christmas dinner. Instead of store-bought gifts, make gifts or share a personal gift such as time or abilities. Instead of ham or turkey with all the trimmings, make a hearty meal of spaghetti or macaroni and cheese together. On December 25, you may be sur-

prised how much better you feel about what you have done—and how delighted you are with your handmade, personal gifts.

Reaching Out to Others

This holiday season, would your family consider lending a hand to others in the name of Christ? Just imagine what the whole bunch of you could accomplish working together for a few hours! You could paint the church fellowship hall; send out potentially lifesaving information for your local Cancer Society; or collect eyeglasses, frames, hearing aids, and precious metal scraps for organizations such as the Lions Club or New Eyes for the Needy (Short Hills, NJ 07078). With a little help from folks just like you, Books Abroad (Box 370, Elkhart, IN 46515) has gathered thousands of books for struggling libraries all over the world.

Adopt-a-Family

One woman, Californian Carol Parker, shared a wonderful project that her family discovered. She explained that, for several years, her family contacted a nonprofit organization called the Box Project. Founded in 1962 by Mrs. Martin Luther King, Jr., this organization matches families nationwide with needy families in the South. The Parkers then "adopted" a family in rural Mississippi that was living below the poverty level, sending them much-needed help and gifts. Mrs. Parker commented that the relationship her family developed with the Mississippi family blossomed, and now they help their adopted family year-round. (For example, when the Parker family realized there weren't any Christmas gifts

they really needed or wanted, they decided to use the money to pay the Mississippi family's utility bill.)

For details on such a project, send a self-addressed stamped envelope to: Box Project, P.O. Box 435, Plainville, CT 06962.

Secret Santa

One family discovered, purely by accident, a way to act as a "Secret Santa" for others. The father of the family noticed a neighbor gazing into a store window, where gay decorations and colorful toys could be seen. Knowing times were tough for this particular neighbor, the father dropped in for a visit. When he did so he discovered that there would be no money for gifts for the small daughter in the household. Impulsively, the father gave his neighbor some money, though his own family really could not spare it. He went home and explained what he had done, and the family was surprised that, somehow, they really did not miss the money. In fact, they had a very nice Christmas despite the financial "loss." As a result, this family decided that every Christmas season they would seek out someone in need and remember that person with a gift given anonymously.

Your family could find great satisfaction in doing likewise. As Secret Santas, you could watch all year long for just the right person to remember at Christmas. The gift need not always be given to the financially needy. Sometimes you may want to reach out to people who are lonely or are experiencing sorrow. You may know your chosen recipient well, or you may choose a stranger. Whatever you do, be sure to remain unknown.

Adopt-a-Newborn

Maybe you can get your family or church to help "adopt" a newborn. This would be an especially fun project for a children's Sunday school class. Locate a needy family or single mother in your church or community who is expecting a baby sometime near Christmas. Have everyone in your church, class, or family join in to build a supply of baby gifts, including hand-crocheted blankets and sweater sets, a playpen pad, layette clothes, diapers, powder, cream, a tiny hairbrush, bottles, nipples—everything the baby will need. Put gifts in a large basket, and, if your church is involved, place an empty cradle under the sanctuary tree so that people can add things all through Advent. Then on Christmas Day, gather everything together and deliver it to the mother. When the baby is finally born, you may be rewarded with a picture of your new little "brother" or "sister." This project can even be extended, if you wish, by sending the child gifts during the year.

Adopt-a-Parish

Why not suggest that your church adopt a poorer parish at Christmas? If there seems to be a shortage of people to head up the project, why don't you volunteer? Write the names and requests of children from the poorer parish on small cards, then hang them on your church's tree. Inform your church members that these children's names are up for grabs by anyone who wants to help. One woman says that at her church, beautifully wrapped gifts begin to appear under the tree many weeks before Christmas. Even small children and the elderly help out by bringing canned

and dried foods. Volunteers take everything to the other parish on December 24.

Catherine Marshall's Family Adoption Project

In *Guideposts* magazine, Catherine Marshall shared how her family discovered a special way to make Christmas more meaningful.

Several years ago the question came up in one of our family sessions: How could the coming Christmas be made more meaningful? And it was the children who, as usual, went right to the heart of the matter: We had to find some way to think more about others.

"I think we should find a poor family and help them," said Jeff, our youngest. It was a good idea—but which poor family? Then one of us happened to mention the Stowes (not their real name), and instantly we were all excited. Actually the Stowes were not poverty-stricken; Mr. Stowe was a schoolteacher, but as such he symbolized to us all those respected citizens who serve selflessly and often with small pay. The Stowes had five children; they lived in a house much too small for such a large family; they were always to be counted on for community projects; and yet they never had those 'extras' that many people take for granted.

"Could we give a present to each one?" Chester asked.

"At least," said Linda, "Maybe several."

"Clothes?" suggested Jeff, though actually he had toys and food more clearly in mind.

It was my husband Len who suggested that the Stowes not be told where the proposed gifts came from. Len was

77

thinking of the theme of Lloyd Douglas's *Magnificent Obsession,* of the power that flows from giving anonymously.

That very day we gave ourselves research assignments. There was detective work to be done on clothing sizes, on the particular wishes and fancies of the five Stowe children. We set up a large cardboard box in the living room, and gradually, as Christmas neared, the box began to fill with presents. For Mrs. Stowe I bought a silk slip, lingerie I suspected she would never treat herself to; and without telling me, Len had a similar idea for Mr. Stowe—a handsome sports shirt. Gently, ever so reverently, the boys placed their own special gifts in the box—baseballs autographed by their particular major-league idols. So it went—clothes and games, toys and eats, personal treasures right up to the top.

Last of all came one of the few anonymous letters I have ever written. In it I explained to the Stowes that the point of the gifts was to try to say to them what their own unselfish giving meant to one family, as well as to others in the community.

Then on Christmas Eve came the most exciting time of all. Our whole family climbed into the station wagon and drove to the Stowes', where furtively and breathlessly . . . we left the box on the Stowe doorstep and cut out—but fast—for home! I have marveled at how the excitement of giving can transform the atmosphere in our home to thoughtfulness, consideration, and love.

Every year as Christmas seems to come faster than ever, every year when that glorious event catches us all but unprepared for its surge of warmth and generosity, I am

convinced that a family project can add a new dimension to family solidarity and new emphasis to what the Babe of Bethlehem means to the world.*

More Helping Ideas

Here are some ideas for reaching out that are outside the regular channels of Christmas giving. They are adapted from an article, "Give unto Others," which I wrote for *Family Circle* magazine:

Invite a Newcomer

Invite a stranger to dinner, maybe someone who has no other place to go, such as a young woman from a halfway house, a truck driver whose work has left him in your city over the holidays, a couple who just moved into the neighborhood, a foreign student. If opening your door to strangers seems difficult, try getting several couples from your neighborhood, club, or church to join you.

Y'all Come

For a really new and effective idea, try "tithing" your holiday dinner invitations. Wouldn't you find great satisfaction in sending one of ten invitations to someone who needs to be with others over the holidays? Not sure who to invite? How about folks living in a homeless shelter, abused wives and children, or struggling non-English speaking immigrants? Remember Jesus' words in Luke 14:12-13, "When you put on a dinner, . . . invite the poor, the crippled, the lame, and the blind." Maybe one or two other families from your church or club would enjoy helping.

*Reprinted with permission from *Guideposts* magazine. Copyright © 1969 by Guideposts Associates, Inc., Carmel, NY, 10512.

Another possibility would be to invite a foreign-exchange student into your home. A Japanese girl who visited in one American home during the holidays volunteered to make an oriental meal for all of them. You may enjoy the company of delightful new people so much that your family will decide to become hosts for International Youth Exchange. If you are interested in this outreach, send for "One Friendship at a Time," a sixty-eight-page booklet that outlines thirty programs for high school and college students and other young adults. The address: Your Guide to International Youth Exchange, Consumer Information Center, Dept. 501P, Pueblo, CO 81009.

The Holiday Project

Add a heartwarming new dimension to your family's celebration: Get involved with the Holiday Project, a national nonprofit organization that brings people together to visit shut-ins in hospitals, nursing homes, and shelters. Write to The Holiday Project, P.O. Box 6829, Dept FC, FDR Station, New York, NY 10150.

Adopt-a-Prisoner

Remember the children of prisoners in your area. These youngsters often are alone and lonely at Christmas and have little hope of receiving even essentials, let alone such gifts as toys. For information on ways to help children of prisoners, write to Prison Fellowship Angel Tree, P.O. Box 17500, Washington, DC 20041.

Letters to Men and Women in the Service

Spend a couple of Advent evenings together as a family writing out Christmas or Hanukkah cards and letters to lonely people in the armed forces who are stationed in faraway places. This can be a wonderful boost to servicemen and women, helping them to remember that folks back home care for and support them. Watch December issues of your local newspaper for APO addresses or call a nearby military post. Commanding officers report many smiles and tears of joy as mail has been distributed on Christmas Eve in years past.

The Super Gifts: Organ Donation Pledges

Fill out an organ donor pledge card. Last year fifty thousand people received organ and tissue donations. "But," says an official at The Living Bank, "there are people waiting for transplants whose time runs out—truly a senseless tragedy when one considers that enough organs will be buried today to supply all those who have a critical need." Find out how to give your wish the force of law by phoning your local driver's license bureau, hospital, or state department of health. Or contact The Living Bank at 1-800-528-2971, or write the American Council on Transplantation (700 N. Fairfax, Suite 505, Alexandria, VA 22314).

Another lifesaving gift would be to donate blood. The American Red Cross literally begs for help in December when demand for plasma is greater because of extended holiday travel and corresponding accidents. Donating is completely safe for healthy people and takes less than an hour. Look in your phone book for the number of the nearest donation center, or call any hospital.

Simple Acts of Kindness

Here are some additional ideas for simple ways to reach out and bless others in Christ's name.

1. Volunteer to work a few hours a week at a local nursing home or hospital. Or phone the county department of human resources and offer to take welfare patients for doctor visits or to deliver food and packages for needy families.

2. Learn sign language so that, with your help, the hearing-impaired can "listen" to Sunday services at your church. Or volunteer to teach an illiterate person to read. Call your local library or contact the Literacy Center at 1-800-228-8813.

3. Let each person choose one name from a list of lonely folks and make an unexpected phone call of encouragement.

4. Let a suffering person know that you will be praying for him or her at seven o'clock each morning (do not forget to do it!) during the Twelve Days of Christmas. Send along a basket of small wrapped gifts at the same time to be opened one per day so the person will remember and be encouraged by your daily prayer support.

Dollars that Do Double Duty

If you have no time to get involved in charity projects, then at least let your gift-buying dollars work overtime by purchasing from charitable organizations, such as church bazaars, nonprofit agencies, outlets for products made by the blind, or other sources set up to help people help themselves. For aid in locating a self-help crafts group in your area, write Southern Highland Handcrafts Guild

and Folk Art Center, P.O. Box 9545, Asheville, NC 28815. Two such groups are Self-help Crafts, 240 N. Reading Road, Ephrata, PA 17522, a relief and service program of the Mennonite Central Committee, and SERRV Self-help Handcrafts, P.O. Box 365, New Windsor, MD 21776, a Church of the Brethren outreach program that purchases craft items from forty countries. The Artisans Cooperative, P.O. Box 216, Chadd's Ford, PA 19317 will send a catalog for one dollar showing handcrafted toys, quilts, potholders, and many other items made by artisans all over America.

Your family can also purchase Christmas cards from charitable organizations or buy holly wreaths from organizations like the Boys Republic of California, so that attention is not centered solely on themselves and church. If you want to send greetings that are more than just pretty, the following groups feature beautiful fund-raising cards:

National Audubon Society
950 Third Avenue
New York, NY 10022

National Wildlife Federation
1412 Sixteenth Street, NW
Washington, DC 20036

Sierra Club
730 Polk Street
San Francisco, CA 94109

UNICEF
331 E. 38th Street
New York, NY 10016

Giving Money Away at Christmas

Do you feel pulled in different directions when it comes to donating your holiday money gifts? Ask your pastor for the name of a needy family. Look around for places where floods, storms, or fires have destroyed homes. Find out what people need, and supply what you can. Ask your local church's benevolence or missions chairman about projects the denomination recommends. Give, but give wisely.

If you have doubts about an organization, call the local Better Business Bureau. Or you can write to the National Charities Information Bureau (19 Union Square West, New York NY 10003) for a booklet titled "Wise Giving Guide" and up to three free reports on specific charities. These reports will detail how much of each dollar donated goes to the cause itself and how much goes to administrative expenses.

Since Christmas is so often equated with children, maybe organizations that deal specifically with children would interest your family the most. It is a sad fact that there are plenty of children who need help of all kinds. Consider this poem, "Sidewalk Lullaby," written by Shari Miller of Teguclgalpa, Honduras:

> Tonight the children of no one
> Will say their prayers on the street;
> They will kneel to hollow god—Hunger;
> The shadows around tuck them in. *

Perhaps you can allow the children to pick an organization that helps poor youngsters worldwide. Could you make it a monthly commitment? Here are a few organizations that help needy children throughout the world:

*Reprinted from *Living More with Less* by permission of Herald Press. All rights reserved.

World Vision Childcare
Arcadia, CA 91006

Everychild
P.O. Box E
Scottsdale, AZ 85252

Futures for Indian Children
4401 Montgomery Blvd. NE
Albuquerque, NM 87109

Save the Children Federation
48 Wilton Road
Westport, CT 06880

Compassion International
3955 Cragwood Dr.
P.O. Box 7000
Colorado Springs, CO 80933

Christian Children's Fund, Inc.
Box 26511
Richmond, VA 23261

Here is a list of organizations that help the homeless. Most are in need of volunteer help as well as money:

National Coalition for the Homeless
1439 Rhode Island Avenue NW
Washington, DC 20005

National Volunteer Hotline
1345 Euclid Street NW
Washington, DC 20002

National Low Income Housing Coalition
1012 14th Street, NW
Suite 1006
Washington, DC 20005

Habitat for Humanity
Habitat and Church Streets
Americus, GA 31709

THREE

Christmas Is Family

Activities that place family
members and friends side-by-side
to help them enjoy each other

Yule traditions do not necessarily have to be religious to reap spiritual results. Enjoying the simplest activity with someone who really wants you nearby can bring a bubbling stream of joy that gives kids (and parents, too!) the priceless gift of feeling that they belong. Youngsters quickly discover what is important to their parents by the activities in which the parents are involved. How much more wonderful it would be for parents to share a circle of friendship and frolic with their children during the Christmas season rather than focusing their energies on buying expensive gadgets to "entertain."

Not sure where you can go or what you can do to capture some sparkling hours of fun and laughter for your family? Here are some fresh togetherness suggestions, gathered from many moms and dads, that will help keep the family glow in Christmas, put hearts in a mellow mood, and make everybody think, *Yes, our family really does the holidays up right.*

Enjoy the Winter Wonderland

Jack Frost may nip at your nose, but get everybody outdoors anyway and have at it! You will find endless delight in making snow angels, eating snow cones, or going sledding, tobogganing, or ice skating "for the kids' sake"—kids of all ages, that is. Find a place in the country that offers horse-drawn sleigh rides or cross-country skiing. (One family spent a Saturday skiing down sidewalks in a local park after a heavy snowstorm.) Or gather up a few hearty players to build forts and have a rough-and-tumble snowball fight. (Careful, though! Be sure to lay down rules for safe play.)

Snow Fun

Snow is a wonderful tool for play. You can make snow angels by dropping on your back in the snow, then sweeping your arms and legs up and down, in and out. Stand up carefully and look at the wonderful angel you have just created.

If your thermometer is dipping below freezing, you can also make snow sculptures. Simply fill an empty appliance carton with snow and let it sit outdoors for about twenty-four hours. When you lift the box away, you'll have a nice solid block of snow for sculpting. As you progress, keep the bottom portion of your sculpture broad. Use a hoe or trowel for preparing the block and then use finer tools like chisels and a putty knife to complete the work. What piece of sculpture do you want to make? An animal? A snow castle? Mickey Mouse? Do not forget to preserve your snow art on film for posterity. Maybe a neighbor can be the judge and a prize offered for best statue. With any cold weather luck, your snow creation will last a long while and you can be sure others on your street will admire this novel way to celebrate Christmas.

Bonus Idea 1: Enjoy a snowflake trap. Paste or staple a piece of dark felt (deep blue makes a beautiful display) on cardboard and let it chill either outdoors or in the freezer for several hours so that flakes will not melt right away when they land on it. If you choose a day when snow is light and dry, the wonderfully unique shapes of falling snowflakes will show better on the felt and remain quite a while. Use a magnifying glass for observation.

This is a marvelous opportunity to discuss spiritual matters casually with children, especially the greatness of our God who can

create such remarkable variety that no two snowflakes are exactly alike. Perhaps the conversation can continue briefly with a comparison of the wonderful uniqueness of each individual in God's world, where no two human beings are exactly alike in appearance, talents, or personality.

Bonus Idea 2: Wipe the snow off of a backyard patio table or brick fence and set up an outdoor snowball shoot. Fill six or so empty plastic bottles or cans about half-full of water, then screw the covers back on and line them up. Have each person throw snowballs, allowing three trys to knock the bottles over. Each knockdown counts as a point; the winner is the first to score twenty-seven. Be sure everybody stands behind a line to make it all fair. If you have enough people, try matching two teams against each other. Or set up a water pistol shoot using styrofoam or paper cups as targets. Let the kids keep score by marking each hit in the snow with a stick.

Gathering the Greenery

If you feel like hiking in the woods, look for different kinds of evergreen trees and bring home samples to staple on cardboard for a holiday display. This could become a nice conversation piece when guests visit. Use a book to identify and compare Scotch pine, cedar, etc. Or gather up pinecones, evergreen branches, red berry clumps, sweet gum balls, and acorns. Then bend a wire coat hanger into a circle and glue your treasures on to make a wreath. If you have an abundance of pinecones around, gather a basketful of all sizes and shapes. Spray them with an adhesive (available in craft stores) and sprinkle on different colors of glit-

ter. When they are dry, dump your cones back into the basket for a delightful, sparkly addition to any decor.

Bonus Idea: Establish an annual sunrise picnic. Take along bacon, eggs, potatoes (canned will do), an old frying pan, a coffee percolator you don't care about, and plastic dishes and silverware. The kids can gather twigs and sticks to build a fire while adults peel potatoes, prepare the coffee, and set the table. Can't you almost catch a whiff of coffee percolating and bacon frying outdoors? Of course, bacon drippings will be used to fry the eggs and potatoes. After breakfast, there will be woods and pleasant trails to investigate, and beautiful bird songs and squirrel and chipmunk antics to enjoy.

Another time, a twilight backyard picnic might be just as much fun, especially on a clear night. When stomachs are filled, lay some blankets on the grass, flop on your backs, and with Dad's help (and a good astronomy book), pick out various stars and constellations in the heavens.

Yule Log Hunt

If you have a big open fireplace and live near a large woods, take your picnic and a big thermos of hot chocolate and let everybody go searching for a real Yule log. It should be hardwood, oversized, and knotty. If it is a bit watersoaked, that is even better. (Europeans say that the finder of the Yule log will have good fortune!) Bring your log home and set it aside while you build a roaring fire in the fireplace (roast chestnuts, too, if you like). When the flames are at their peak, lay the Yule log on the fire. Tradition dictates that (1) as long as the log burns, sometimes two or three

days, all nonessential work will be banned (the kids will adore this part!) and (2) one burned-out piece must be saved to throw on with the dry kindling to start next year's fire. Some families place a smaller Yule log on the mantel instead, drilling twelve holes in it and placing a white candle in each hole. Every evening during the Twelve Days of Christmas, one more candle is lit.

Tap a Tree

Got a maple tree you can tap? You need only a generous snowfall and a single ingredient, maple syrup, to make snow candy (if you don't have a tree, simply purchase the syrup at the grocery store). Boil a cup of syrup for about five minutes or until thickened. Fill a two-quart, heat-proof bowl with clean snow and drizzle the hot syrup over it. Voilà! Delicious hard-rock maple candy that you can pick up and eat with your fingers.

Families Going Places

You'll never find a better time for family fun than Christmas. Children are home from school, and working moms and dads usually have a day or two off. So why not take advantage of the time with some family outings? When you are ready to say to the kids, "OK, let's go!" here are some ideas that can lead to wonderful traditions as rich as Christmas itself.

Christmas Open House

Visit an open house or a nearby mansion that allows visitors. During the holidays, many communities lavishly decorate public places and offer elegant candlelight tours. The governor's home in Atlanta, Georgia, features several evenings of caroling around

the tree in the library with eighteenth-century costumed ladies as greeters and a white-wigged harpsichordist to accompany the singing. At Atlanta's Callenwold, the Christmas open house raises money for the center's fine arts programs. A different designer is invited to decorate each room of the gracious 1920s Tudor mansion in a distinctively glorious holiday mood. The Winterthur Museum in Wilmington, Delaware, offers an eighteen-foot tree decorated entirely with dried flowers.

Check with your local chamber of commerce to find out what wonders are waiting for you and your family in or near your own hometown.

Community Decoration Adventure

Take the family for a walk or drive around the neighborhood to view the beautiful decorations and lawn displays. Would your family enjoy a little contest to see who can jot down the most Christmas symbols seen? Examples: the cross, the fish design of early Christians, bells that peal out the message of Christ's birth, candles that show forth Christ as the Light of the World, greenery that bespeaks life and Jesus' resurrection from the dead, and angels that remind us of the heavenly host near Bethlehem. Perhaps your community has its own traditional outdoor display like the night parade of lighted sailing yachts on the inland waterway at West Palm Beach, Florida.

Christmas Story Hours

Take young children to the library for Christmas story hours. Children and adults alike will enjoy listening to wonderfully willing and talented workers as they read Christmas stories and clas-

sics aloud. Or you could take the family to a local showing of *The Nutcracker* or *Amahl and the Night Visitors.*

Newborn Visit

Many young children have never seen a newborn. In December, why not take your youngsters to visit the local hospital nursery during regular visiting hours. What better way could there be to show them what the baby Jesus might have looked like?

Shopping Date with the Kids

Make a shopping date with your child. Let each parent take one youngster separately for an excursion at the most wonderfully exciting department store you can think of. The goal? To discover the perfect gift for someone special. While it is important to do things as a family, every child needs individual attention, too, especially during bustling December days when kids' needs can easily get overlooked. Have youngsters draw names for this special night out, and watch their eyes light up when you offer a little bonus spending money! Maybe the family photobug can snap a picture just before each trip and get an "arms loaded" shot when parent and child return.

The Ultimate Christmas Family Vacation

Plan a once-in-a-lifetime Christmas family vacation. Find out all you can about some intriguing place that interests everyone. In January, have a family meeting to decide where you will go, then encourage everybody to put away 20 percent of allowances all year for a memorable holiday weekend at a spa, ski lodge, or a

place such as Sturbridge, Massachusetts, where being snow-bound in a quaint New England village could be a holiday dream come true. Or what about Williamsburg, Virginia, where Christmas is celebrated in authentic early American tradition? Wherever you go, be sure to capture every wonderful moment on film. You may even want to appoint certain family members as "trip recorders," to take pictures, gather souvenirs, and keep a journal.

The Greening

There's nothing quite so wonderful and exciting as a Christmas tree, and it doesn't really matter whether it's real or artificial! Christmas trees add something special to the spirit and atmosphere of Christmas. This year, make a big deal of your family Christmas tree. You may find that this is a delightful way to draw your family closer together during this hectic holiday season.

The Search for the Perfect Tree

If possible, gather the children to help choose and cut a fresh evergreen from a nearby tree farm. (Perhaps you can cut two trees and deliver the extra to a family that cannot afford to buy its own.) Our children loved running up and down the rows of trees, pointing out the nicest and biggest ones, and then helping draw the saw across the trunk and pulling the chosen one out of the lot to be set up in our living room. Take along a lunch to eat outdoors, or serve the same traditional menu each year after you get back home. How about clam chowder? Steaming hot homemade vegetable soup? Fruit cake and punch? Pizza? Or serve fresh

apple cake after the last stocking is hung just because that is the way you always did it back home.

Trim-a-Tree Festivities

Be as creative as you can with your tree-trimming festivities. Have an ornament hunt for preschoolers—searching for the shiny treasures will help keep these little ones busy and happy while the older children and adults hang the lights. Play background holiday music while you pull decorations from boxes and bags and hang them first here, then there, on the tree. If the whole gang is gathered, there will be arranging and rearranging and lots of giggling as everybody wants to suggest the best place for each ornament. In our house, when the mistletoe was hung for hugs and kisses and the tree topped off with Grandma's gold-braided antique angel, everyone shouted a loud "Hooray" and ran for the hot chocolate brewing on the stove top. Don't you just love to watch the wonder and delight on the children's faces when the room is darkened and the colorful lights are turned on?

Bonus Idea 1: Children almost always enjoy a small tree in their own bedrooms to decorate any way they wish. Offer prizes for the most beautiful, most imaginative, most creative, cutest, or whatever fits your family. There could be just as many prizes offered as there are children so no one gets left out on Christmas morning when awards are made by Mom and Dad. Homemade blue, green, or red ribbons can be hung on winners' bedroom doors and will likely be enough of a prize.

Bonus Idea 2: Looking for an inexpensive way to make your tree look beautifully distinctive? A military family with relatives scattered all over the world can place small flags on their tree to represent countries where other family members reside or, perhaps, where they have lived while Dad has been in the country's service. A family that has hosted foreign exchange students for years can put up flags representing their guests' various homelands: Belgium, France, Mexico, Sweden, or whatever. Each student would probably enjoy a color photo of the international tree. A "crafty" mom whose relatives come from Europe can crochet and starch small lacy doilies that resemble snowflakes and hang them next to fresh oranges tied to branches with slender red ribbons, because that is what folks do in Europe.

Bonus Idea 3: Maybe you can keep a single color scheme for your tree. In New England for instance, it is popular to spray the tree white, symbolizing the pristine purity of the Christ child and the cleanness of the saints before God because of Christ's complete sacrifice on the cross. The White Christmas theme is continued by tying on hundreds of white velvet bows and fabric roses, white felt angels, foam stars, sprayed white apples, painted wooden crosses, small white tissue-wrapped gifts, or by draping on garlands of white beads.

Family Memory Tree

For a Christmas tree that will take center stage at any gathering, hang family memorabilia as ornaments. Just watch the children run to the tree as soon as they come in the door, searching for

their very own first pair of baby booties and rattles, a beloved toy balsam airplane, a seashell from a beach vacation, Mom and Dad's wedding snapshot, Great-granny's necklace, a pressed flower from a prom bouquet, or a Sunday school good-attendance pin. A mother can arrange a grown-up daughter's first dolls, an old and exquisite hand-built dollhouse, a married son's train set, or a favored toy and truck set into a still life beneath the tree. Priceless nostalgic decorations such as these will provoke cheery chatter and reminiscences and serve as reminders of the love and care in the lives of the family.

Scandinavian Table Tree

Scandinavians often fashion a traditional table tree from slender varnished wood strips (see drawing) and stick it into a pretty flowered dirt pot. Children then string on fresh-baked gingerbread

figures, wrapped in cellophane, and push apples onto the ends of the "branches." Sometimes folks from Norway, Denmark, and Sweden push evergreen nests into wicker baskets that will hold the biggest and reddest polished apples available. They then set the baskets, small and large, beside the tree, next to the front door in the vestibule, or on the mantel or dining-room table. These are real showpieces with natural red and green Christmas colors!

International Tree

A woman I know who travels worldwide enjoys buying small souvenirs to use as Christmas tree ornaments. Friends and relatives know her hobby, too, and often "gift" her with unique figures throughout the year. "Each one takes on a special meaning and brings back a flood of fond memories as I decorate the tree," she says.

Do you have some reminders or souvenirs of places you have visited? Why not gather them together and create your own international tree? This could be a beautiful and delightful way to display your treasures and spark many happy memories.

Gumdrop Tree

It takes only a few minutes to make a gumdrop tree. Stick toothpicks through green leaf gumdrops and into a styrofoam cone. Place smaller gumdrops of various colors here and there to resemble tree lights. You can make a whole forest of these sugar'n'spice child-pleasers for a candyland display on your mantel and coffee tables. Or you could use the best one as a centerpiece for the Christmas dinner table. Just watch these delectable

edibles disappear when you end the meal by passing around the sweets!

You can also decorate a pretty table tree all over with incredible edibles, like marzipan candy, colorful wrapped peppermints, or homemade fudge squares. Then invite visitors and party guests to help themselves.

December Meals at Home

Make a firm commitment to eat morning and evening meals together as much as you can during the month of December. "The family that eats together, speaks together," says family life worker Beth Riley. Writing in *Mississippi Today* (November 1986), she notes:

> People don't eat together enough to talk at all. Dinner at my parents' house meant everyone crowding into our tiny kitchen to sit around the table. When we moved to a larger house, we kept the dining room for Sunday. But the kitchen couldn't accommodate a table and violà!—the countertop eating area was introduced into our lives. Nobody faced anyone at the breakfast bar and we were pretty uncomfortable perched on those bar stools, so we ate quickly and left. Soon, we were eating at different times. . . . Since food is a necessity for humans, why not take the mealtime and turn it into 'quality time'? It doesn't take an impossible effort to prepare a meal and serve it with some dignity.

Don't let your family mealtimes escape you, especially during the Christmas holidays. Instead, look through the following ideas for ways to make your meals a time of sharing and warmth.

December Delight Meal

Get everybody involved in a weekly December Delight meal. Each person takes responsibility for one dish they love—soup, salad, casserole, homemade bread, dessert, or whatever. Younger children will love making boxed pudding or Jell-O desserts, and everybody gets to eat a favorite dish.

Family Fun-Time Placemats

Order Family Fun-Time placemats from Sweet Publishing Company (Fort Worth, TX 76137.) Use those with Yule themes to prompt interesting mealtime conversation about making the Bible practical. All of these placemats contain favorite Bible stories and family fun activities. Hopefully, everyone will enjoy these times together enough to commit to regular daily devotions after the holidays.

Bake Yourselves Happy

Lovers of sweets, rejoice! Christmas is just the right time for families to get together in the kitchen to bake up scrumptious holiday treats. There are bound to be yummy, gooey pans to lick and plenty of tasty treats for everybody. Even the littlest angels will be willing to help out. Best of all, you will be able to surprise folks on your Christmas list with baskets full of homemade irresistibles, such as holiday quick breads, muffins, chocolate macaroons, soft pretzels, and other savory delights. Or, use your goodies to plan a cookie swap with other families (see page 117).

Take the kids shopping with you to help select the ingredients for your merry treats. Then involve them with the stirring and mixing and kneading and cutting. Borrow recipes from friends,

neighbors, and grandparents, and invest in wonderfully appealing teddy-bear-shaped cake tins, mini-muffin pans, and maybe a rolling pin cookie mold. What about purchasing a set of cookie cutter stars, graduated in size, so you can frost, decorate and stack cookies to resemble a deliciously festive Christmas tree? Or, make cookies and put names on them with frosting, then use them as placecards for the Christmas dinner table. There will be excited chatter and plenty of family camaraderie as children gain valuable hands-on kitchen experience and get to decorate their own creations. (When frosted by little hands, some treats will turn out purple and black—but not to worry! All creations will be pretty enough to serve with hot wassail for a holiday open house.)

For simple recipes to make with children, check out one or more of the following: *The New Junior Cookbook* (Better Homes and Gardens); *My First Cookbook* by Angela Wilkes (Alfred A. Knopf); *Kids' Microwave Munchies* (Reynolds Wrap Kitchens, Richmond, VA 23261-2003); *My First Cookbook* by Rena Coyle (Workman Publishing Co.); *Please Cook with Children* (compiled and published by the Please Touch Museum for Children in Philadelphia).

Old-Fashioned Taffy Pull

Here's an idea for some real kitchen fun: Get everybody together for an old fashioned taffy pull. Wrap your terrific little taffy treats individually in wax paper, twist the ends, and share them with everybody you see. Tie on tiny bright bows and use some for tree or package decorations. Pack a dozen in a little basket to give as a gift to a next-door neighbor, or set a tempting bowlful by the front door to welcome guests.

 *Bonus Idea:* Make candied apples. Their bright red color makes them delectable holiday favorites. Happy holidays and all that good stuff!

Candlelight Extravaganzas

May every twinkling star you see this season, every shining candle and every blazing Yule log, be for you an invitation: "Jesus Christ is born. Come near the Light of the World and get warm."*

My big splurge has always been buying dozens of red and white candles, tall and short ones, rotund and tapered ones, to light up every nook and cranny of our house for several evenings before Christmas. When the children saw me getting out the candles, they would always scrounge in the bottom of the toy box for wood alphabet blocks to spell N-O-E-L and W-E L-O-V-E C-H-R-I-S-T-M-A-S to place atop the mantel.

At dusk, I would fill our three antique kerosene lamps with colored oil and make them come alive by striking a match. Sometimes I would place a votive candle inside a four-sided vegetable grater as a centerpiece on the dining room table. The twinkles coming through the holes looked like starlight to the children. The gentle flickering glow cast a quiet and peaceful light, as if from another era.

Younger children always love to stand and gaze at the extravaganza of silent flickering lights. They enjoy sitting together with one adult or another in the mellow glow to talk, listen to carols, or read stories. In our family it was a favorite holiday pastime. When

*Reprinted with permission from Resource Publications, Inc., 160 E. Virginia St., Suite 290, San Jose, CA 95112.

it is time for bed, maybe your kids, too, will run to get a candle snuffer (in our case, it was Grandma's treasured sterling silver candle snuffer) and take turns extinguishing the flames.

Candle hints:

1. Spray vegetable oil inside candle holders so the stubs will slip out easily.

2. If a good candle becomes crooked, place it in hot water for about ten minutes, then stick a safety pin through the wick and hang it up on a hook to straighten.

3. Run out of candle holders? Use muffin tins, stemware, glass tumblers, or small pots filled with gravel or dirt.

4. Keep candle wax, which is difficult to remove, from getting on the tablecloth by cutting a drip catcher three inches in diameter from a white plastic meat tray. Cut a hole in the center to slip the candle through. For a decorative touch, use pinking shears.

Gala December Family Evenings

Enjoying just one or two planned evenings together can make December a standout in most families. Here are some ideas.

Making Butter

Do homespun things, such as making butter. Whip heavy cream, or take turns shaking it in a tightly covered jar. If you have one, use an old fashioned butter churn. Perhaps you could make apple butter or boil up a batch of the kids' favorite jam. Do you remember eating deep-fat-fried, sugar-dusted rosette crullers at county

fairs and carnivals? Batter irons and recipes for these easy treats are still available in kitchenware departments of most department stores. Let everyone know that kitchen helpers get all they want to eat!

Making Soap or Candles

Soap making is easy and requires only ordinary household items, but an adult is definitely needed. Send $2 for an eight-page instruction booklet to RASCO Inc., Box 193, Lakeville, CT 06039. The flyer includes step-by-step recipes for safely making several types of soap, including laundry and complexion soap. Foldout pages discuss coloring and molding.

You can make candles by melting down old candle stubs or broken crayons, then pouring the meltings into tin cans or cardboard milk or juice cartons. A good book on this subject is *Candle-making* by Susanne Strose (Sterling Publishing Co.) For a catalog of unique molds and other candle-making supplies, write Barker Enterprises, 15106 10th Avenue SW, Seattle, WA 98166.

Fun and Games

Plan an evening of fun and games playing Scrabble, Flinch, Sorry, Clue, Pit, Trivial Pursuit, checkers, charades, or some other favorite. You can even keep one game like Monopoly going on and on, picking up exactly where you left off every time. Another idea would be to organize a dart, Ping-Pong, or marbles tournament and put up a wall chart to keep track of star players or teams.

Craft Night

Plan a family crafts evening. Enlist everybody to help make decorations, customized wrapping paper, greeting cards, or Yule banners. Maybe you can let each person be responsible for fashioning a dozen yarn flowers on a daisy wheel to be crocheted together in an afghan by Mom or Big Sister after the holidays. Perhaps you could work together to tie a quilt that Mom pieced together years ago. When it is done, place names in a hat and have a drawing to see who uses the gorgeous piece on their bed.

Whatever craft project you choose, be sure everybody gathers for a celebration when it is completed.

Stargazing

An evening of stargazing can be a delight for the entire family. You all can wonder together about the Christmas star and the glories of the universe as you wander out under God's sky. Use a constellation chart from a library book or an almanac that shows moon phases and tells which planets are visible. Or, write for these three free booklets—"Comets," "Meteorites," and "Life in the Universe"—from the Public Affairs Office, Harvard Smithsonian Center for Astrophysics, 60 Garden Street, Cambridge, MA 02138.

Even small youngsters can easily locate such familiar constellations as Orion and the Big Dipper and find the Milky Way. Choose a clear night, preferably someplace away from city streetlights. Why not rent a telescope for added excitement? (If your family enjoys science projects, order a Smithsonian Family Learning Project Science Calendar for about $13. These calendars suggest intriguing experiments that parents and kids can do

together. Calendars can be ordered from GMG Publishing, 25 W. 43rd Street, New York, NY 10036.)

"Best Christmas Gift, Worst Christmas Gift" Contest

Alternatives, a not-for-profit organization dedicated to helping people simplify sacred celebrations, sponsored this intriguing contest. One winning "Best Gift" entry came from a death-row prisoner in Mississippi, who received a lovely handmade card with a caring message from a nine-year-old Indian child in Oklahoma. The winning "Worst Gift" entry was submitted by a man whose daughter received a baby Mork doll inside an egg, which was designed to resemble Jesus in a manger. When an attached string was pulled, the toy played a space-age Christmas tune. Think together about the best and worst gifts your family has received or heard about. You may be surprised at how this promotes good humor, as well as discussions about gratitude, greed, Christmas buying excesses, and the real meaning behind Christmas.

Just-to-Say-Hello Evening

This is the night for keeping in touch with friends and relatives who live far away, and to write letters telling the great glad tidings of your family's comings and goings. Just for fun, start off a little crazy by serving breakfast at supper time: bacon, eggs, English muffins, orange juice, coffee, and maybe strawberry pie with whipped cream for dessert. Enlist the kids ahead of time to locate stationery that is unusual, either in design (shaped like an angel or star) or color (yes, red and white checkerboard or zebra striped is OK) or size (why not an oversized family letter on a 24"

x 38" piece of poster board?). Keep the message sensible, though, even if the stationery is outrageous. Consider what the others will be wondering about all of you. Where is Dad working now? What about little Jimmy's diabetes? Did Ted win the track meet? How is Mom's garden doing? Did Jill break off with her boyfriend? Share a few stories about family events (such as the squirrel in the attic or how the baby washed the piano with Comet cleanser). Let the recipients know that personally written letters are your family's gift to their family during the holidays. Stick a couple of recent photographs in each envelope.

Making Maps

Make a relief map of your area using homemade salt-and-flour clay. (To make clay, mix together four cups of flour and one cup of salt with enough water to make a firm but pasty consistency.) Use a pencil or marker to outline mountains, lakes, flatlands, beaches, swamps, and other familiar topography on a piece of plywood or extra-heavy cardboard. Spread on the clay, pressing it with your hands into high peaks and low mounds for mountains and hills, flattening it for plains, pushing down depressions that resemble bodies of water and leaving empty spaces for craters. Let the map dry for about five days. Once your map is dry, use tempera paints to color plains green, rivers and lakes blue, mountains gray or brown. Place a marker where you live and draw in a main highway.

Armchair Travels

Choose a country or state your child would like to learn a lot about, maybe where she was born, where grandparents live, or

where missionary or military friends work. Use encyclopedias, social studies books, travel flyers, and almanacs to find out all you can about the place. Consider such information as how people make a living, what kinds of things children do, what houses are like, and other tidbits of information like favorite foods or famous folks born there. For some real in-depth study, perhaps your family could even plan a trip there next year.

Continuous Holiday Project

What about a continuing family project to last throughout the holidays? Set up an intricate thousand-piece jigsaw puzzle on a coffee or card table to be "absolutely and for sure" completed by Christmas Eve. Enlist everybody in the family to give a hand to meet this very serious deadline, and cheerfully challenge all guests who drop by to take part as well.

Family Photographers

Maybe you can get everybody excited about a special hobby like photography. Older children can go with you to help pick out a new camera and attend a how-to class. Keep film on hand and cash to develop it promptly. Encourage kids to take photos on their own. Appoint a couple of people each week in December as family photographers. It then becomes their duty to capture hilarious, surprising, and satisfying moments. Take snapshots of everybody eating dinner, baking cookies, doing dishes, trimming the tree, etc. Take advantage of the glorious Christmas decorations at shopping malls as backgrounds for snapshots of each other in Sunday-best clothes, then enclose those photos with greeting cards. Request that family members caption, date, and mount their photographic master-

pieces in an album, or have photos made into a mini-scrapbook as a surprise for the family on New Year's.

Five- or Ten-Minute Fun Encounters

These brief togetherness breaks will allow you to "gift" your child with a few minutes of your time during the holiday season.

1. Set the table together

2. Play a game of tiddlywinks, jacks, follow the leader, or Simon says

3. Look at photographs of you as a baby or toddler

4. Give horsey-back rides

5. Color a page in a coloring book together

6. Read a Bible story together, such as Paul's shipwreck (Acts 27)

7. Pot a flower bulb or plant seeds

8. Take a walk in the rain

9. Exchange back rubs or tickles

10. Hide a little surprise and allow the child to search for it

11. Pop popcorn

12. Plan which birthday gift to buy for another family member

13. Cut up two big apples or oranges to share

14. Rock together in the porch swing

15. Work a simple crossword puzzle

16. Talk together about what the child wants to be as an adult

17. Sort clothes and throw a batch into the washer

18. Show the child how to grate cheese for spaghetti, use a garlic press, or make fudge

19. Get down on hands and knees and race little cars on the floor.

Bonus Idea: Make it a tradition to keep time open between Christmas and New Year's (as much as you can) to spend time with the children who are home from school. Maybe you can plan some puttering time just to make yourself available. Try to ignore after-holiday sales, too, no matter how inviting the markdowns may seem. (Unless, of course, the kids really want to go along to spend money they have received!) Keep TV and video viewing to a minimum, too, to extend the peace of Christmas.

You will find that younger children seem to feel snug and comfortable at home, enjoying each others' new playthings and gifts, talking together, and reading by themselves or with adults. This can be a golden opportunity for parents and children to play together, especially if there are new toys and games waiting to be explored. Our college-aged daughters loved spending time gabbing with me in the kitchen, kidding around with their daddy out in the garage, or helping the younger children put together their new toys.

Too often people watch their holidays slip away as they run here and there, trying to make their days "merry and bright" at movies or other events that take them away from home, usually

in opposite directions. We have found that it is much more satisfying to spend time together, staying at home, inviting other families to visit, or going as a family to visit friends.

For some good ideas on spending quality time with your family, read *Let's Make a Memory* by Gloria Gaither and Shirley Dobson (Word Publishers).

Happy Family Entertaining

When good friends, relatives, *and* their children get together and enjoy each other—with or without the best silverware and china—a blessed spirit of love often washes over each person there. Such interaction can give us a new confidence to go about our regular business when the December holidays are long forgotten. We feel appreciated and loved. The following get-together ideas, shared by other families just like yours, will help connect moms, dads, friends, and kids during the Christmas season.

(P.S. It is hard to feel a strong sense of family unity when adults are drinking alcohol. Drinking can make some people feel lethargic and seem uncaring, or even hostile. Drinking alcohol is an activity in which children cannot share. Since this is a family time, in which youngsters are involved, why not keep your holidays dry?)

Christmas Eve Supper

For years, our family made a tradition of going to Grandma's house on the farm on Christmas Eve for oyster stew and crackers. Oysters became synonymous with Christmas Eve. One year a young cousin requested macaroni and cheese or pizza instead.

The firm negative cries from other relatives were heard loud and clear. Tradition reigned. It would be oyster stew or nothing.

Perhaps your family could decide on some special food to have every Christmas Eve. Consider family favorites or a meal that is traditional for your cultural background.

You can do other things, too, to make Christmas Eve a special, memorable time. If your family is quite musical and there is willing talent, sing carols around the piano after supper, or listen to the newer instrumentalists play songs they have been practicing. You may even want to extend your family for this night. Probably nobody would mind if you brought along a friend who needed to be with other people. Somehow, bringing guests adds to the spirit of things—and there is *always* enough food. One year, my mom brought a sad, elderly friend who had been widowed only a little while and needed cheering up. It made us all happier to see her sing carols the loudest of all!

Potluck

You can make meal preparation a breeze for the hostess, ask that every family bring along their choice of a main dish, salad, or dessert. Or you could ask guests to name two dishes they enjoy making, then select one to bring. Just watch those good cooks shine! The day before folks gather, make little toothpick flags that say "Gerry's cranberry sauce" or "Aunt Dee Dee's mincemeat pie" so everyone knows who made what. Usually potlucks turn out like a smorgasbord feast! Even if yours does not, there will be plenty of good eating for all, and so what if there are too many desserts?

One woman assigned everybody to bring along one special ingredient for onion soup. She had the soup pot on the stove as guests arrived (veggies had to be peeled and cut), and dinner was ready an hour later. A potluck pasta party will bring heaping bowls of delicious spaghetti sauce, meatballs, tortellini, and lasagna. For a take-out smorgasbord, ask guests to bring a dish to share from their favorite take-out place, maybe Chinese or French, or a German bakery.

Bonus Idea 1: Ask each family to bring along small wrapped goodies like popcorn packets, homemade jam, or fresh-baked cookies. Tell everyone that a van will be leaving your house after supper for all who want to go caroling. The treats will be dropped off wherever there are folks who look like they need special cheering up.

Bonus Idea 2: Use your holiday get-together to work on a project that will benefit someone else. Tie a quilt for a church raffle or assemble pinecone wreaths and tree ornaments for a church or club bazaar.

If potlucks or dinners aren't your thing, here are some other family party activities.

Talent Fest

Have each invited guest and the children of all ages participate, no matter how amateurish they claim to be. This activity is good for lots of laughs as would-be actors ham it up. A family can pool

talents for a group performance (like the "Hamilton Home Rock and Roll Band") or plan individual activities. Let your third grader exhibit new karate moves he perfected in a beginner's class. Have Big Sister show off difficult gymnastic routines she learned at school. Is somebody good at card tricks? Pantomimes? Playing the trumpet? Telling jokes? Here's your chance to create one star after another with your applause.

Polaroid Scavenger Hunt

Divide guests into three or four groups, then provide each group with a rented or borrowed Polaroid camera. Assign a list of subjects to photograph. The first group to return with a snapshot of every item wins! Limit the time to one or two hours. The list might include Santa Claus, a Christmas tree over eight feet tall, a Salvation Army kettle, a shopper carrying the most packages, a shopper with the biggest package, two turtle doves, or the most beautiful wreath. Afterward, put photos on display for all to see and enjoy.

Caroling Competitions

You will need a group of people and their children who love to sing together, a piano or guitar player, and Christmas sheet music or hymnals for the instrumentalist. The object is to see who remembers more words to the carols so they can hang in there and sing longer than anyone else. Appoint an enthusiastic choral director (anybody who is willing is OK), and a scoring judge, who will eliminate folks who have stopped singing because they forgot the words. First verses will go well. But wait until the second and third stanzas! In each song, the person to outlast the others gains a point, and the

one with the most points at the end wins. You may be surprised to discover that the least likely youngster just may outsing all the others.

Swap Parties

Have a cookie swap party. Admission is a big batch of your finest cookie creations. Tell each guest to bring at least a dozen more than he or she would like to swap and an empty container. That way everybody can eat to their hearts' content and still go home with a delectable assortment. There will be luscious extra-fancy cookies, some lavishly decorated with silvered balls and confetti candy, delicious legendary ethnic recipes, cookies rich with butter and nutmeats; some delicate and lacy and tender, some chewy or crispy, some glazed with velvety frosting that melts in the mouth. The hostess should have her best lace or linen tablecloth on her biggest candlelit table, ready to receive each tempting platterful. Cookies should be covered with see-through plastic for easy viewing. Each plate should be identified with the creator's name and the recipe title. Ask everyone to bring several copies of each recipe to lay beside the plates, free for the taking. Or have the hostess collect these ahead of time and staple together a booklet of recipes for each family to take home. This way, she will also know in advance what everybody is bringing and won't wind up with half a dozen fruit bar plates.

Before tasting begins, ask each family or guest to share a bit about the recipe's history, anything unusual about it, the ease or difficulty of preparation (did the dog eat the first batch, or is some exotic ingredient needed?). There will likely be tales of how secret recipes were passed from generation to generation for a

hundred years, or of winning blue ribbons at county fairs. After each story, pass samples of that particular cookie for all to enjoy.

Note: The hostess can make up an extra batch of cookies for someone who might want to come but did not have enough time to bake. Maybe working friends or others unable to attend could supply cookies and a copy of their recipe, and then drop by later to pick up their tray, now transformed with new varieties and flavors of treats. Imagine the joy! The best part of the cookie exchange is that everybody ends up with a wide variety of delectables.

For a fun twist, insist that all cookies be made by husbands, male friends, or children. Vote by secret ballot to select "best cookie in the house." Winner gets to take home an extra plateful of goodies.

Bonus Idea 1: As a nice variation, plan a book swap party. Every ardent reader knows that there is nothing like reading a good book while snuggled in a comfortable armchair on a cold winter night. Request that each guest (kids too!) bring several hardcover or paperback books (no tacky rejects, please!) to be exchanged. Before the swap, ask each guest to give a two- or three-sentence review of his or her book, then allow everyone to select as many as they brought. Kids can have their own book exchange in an adjoining room.

Bonus Idea 2: Every household seems to own more items than it wants or needs, such as pictures, dishes, costume jewelry, clothing, etc. Have guests bring along several good usable items, unwrapped, to be displayed on a large table. Draw numbers to determine the order in which folks will get to select

an item. Unclaimed treasures can be taken to Goodwill or the Salvation Army.

🐚*Bonus Idea 3:* Invite friends over, asking each to bring a basket or box of about a dozen ornaments they have made or enjoyed using over the years. The more unique the better. Be sure each is tagged with the owner's name and be sure to let guests know that those they bring may be chosen by others to take home. Insides of baskets and boxes can be lined with festive holiday prints or checks. Guests also should bring along scissors and leftover Christmas fabric, ribbon, sequins, and other trims. The hostess can provide assorted small plastic foam shapes, glue, and other scrap supplies. After tea and cookie treats, each guest will spend the evening fashioning two or three new ornaments that will be name-tagged and added to the baskets. Containers are then passed around so everybody can take whatever is appealing, up to the number he or she brought. Each will go home after an evening of fun and fellowship, with tree ornaments that will bring pleasant memories of the original owner for many years ahead.

Open House with Sandbag Luminarias

Your family (kids too!) can host an open house for as many other couples, families, and singles of all ages as you can think of. Luminarias will make the event long remembered. It is simple to make fifty or sixty of these wonderful little lights to line sidewalks and driveways. Dump into a white lunchbag two or three cups of sand. Then firmly press a votive candle down into it. Roll the bag top back about two inches on the outside to form a stiff cuff.

Space the bags outdoors about six to eight feet apart to provide a unique and festive greeting for all who come. If you place candles in the freezer beforehand, most will continue to burn brightly for about three hours, even in a brisk December breeze.

Residents of Tularosa, New Mexico, set out luminarias from one end of town to the other during the holidays to greet motorists passing along the main highway. Signs posted here and there ask drivers to dim headlights so the lovely Christmas candle glow can show better. Most travelers willingly join the celebration by doing just that. Would your townspeople enjoy setting out such an appropriate celebration of the Christ child?

Bonus Idea 1: Advertise in the church or club newsletter that your family is receiving guests on Christmas or New Year's Eve from seven to nine o'clock. Make it clear that children are invited, too. When everybody leaves and everything is in place again, your family can enjoy a quiet time in front of the fireplace waiting for twelve o'clock. Or, you could all attend Midnight Mass or a watchnight service at church.

Bonus Idea 2: Maybe you and your friends don't seem to fit into any group at Christmas, even though you'd like to. Sometimes single parents, widowed folks, or foreign visitors feel like misfits during the holidays because everyone else seems to go home to family. There are many lonely people in big office buildings and department stores or factories. If you are one of these people, why not do something about the situation? Search out a few others who have no nearby family or special place to go, and invite them to spend Christmas Day at your place. Yes, you can do it! Food can be potluck on paper plates and may well turn out

to be a feast. Assign duties like setting the table, washing dishes, and clean up. Never mind that there will be noisy and excited kids underfoot. This is family! Ask parents to bring along games and to provide supplies for making decorations to keep restless youngsters busy. (Some ideas: popcorn and cranberries to string; pinecones and pipe cleaners for wreaths; straws to cut and tie together for stars; colored construction paper, scissors, and paste for cutting out chains and snowflakes or making greeting cards.) Older children and adults will enjoy playing Nintendo, pool, or other games, watching television, not to mention the talk, talk, talk.

Guests can bring along guests, too, maybe a lonely cousin or aunt or someone awaiting a baby in a nearby unwed mothers center. If Joe plays the piano, invite everyone to sing. You may discover another Pavarotti! Can Al do magic tricks? Then let him entertain everybody. New friends will be made and next year, one of the guests may offer to host the gala event. It seems there are more people than ever these days who seem to fit nowhere during the holidays. You may find your lovely group of "square pegs in round holes" will grow so much in years to come that a church or club hall will have to be rented to accommodate everyone. Then won't you be glad you thought of the idea?

Progressive Holiday Party

Link family and friends all evening by offering appetizers at one house, soup and salad at another, a main dish somewhere else, and a grand finale of desserts—to which everyone has contributed—at the final stop. Nobody will have a lot to prepare, and by the end of the evening, your family and friends will have shared a

wonderful meal and several hours of warm friendship in each others' homes. The kids will love the goings and comings, and there will usually be enough food for any houseguests you choose to bring along.

Instant Parties

1. Dial-a-Friend. Call a few friends at the last minute and enjoy the fun of seeing folks arrive "as you are," perhaps in overalls with hammer in hand, or in curlers and pajamas.

2. Christmas Eve Barbecue. One Southern farm family begins roasting a little pig over an open backyard pit about noon on December 24. Guests arrive a few hours later bringing the remaining food and one gift to exchange. Later everyone gathers around a big bonfire for caroling.

Christmas Family Reunions

In the years ahead, Grandma and Grandpa and Aunt Ella may not be around to join the Christmas fun. It may be now or never for an honest-to-goodness reunion of the entire family in the old town where most grew up. What a time everybody could have reminiscing, laughing, singing, and chatting until midnight! In quieter moments, folks can stroll with Mom and Dad by the old homestead, or show the family the church where brass plaques on stained glass windows are dedicated to great grandparents, or take a walk together through the hometown cemetery and let an older relative identify graves of nearly forgotten family members. Sure, some will have to sleep on the floor in sleeping bags or on

couches, and the little ones may be three or four to a bed. Yes, there will be long or short lines for the bathroom . . . but no one will mind. One family I know accommodated forty people this way, each group of ten making their own breakfast in shifts. They sent out for pizza about four-thirty in the afternoon and fixed late night sandwiches at bedtime or whenever they wished. They were together and that is what mattered. Christmas Day, chores were listed on slips of paper and piled in a bowl for everybody to draw one: peel potatoes, prepare the turkey, make dessert, wash salad fixings, clean up afterward, etc. This family found their reunion so exciting that they plan to have another one soon.

Bonus Idea 1: For extra fun, collect a set amount from each family member and have matching T-shirts made up for everybody to wear during the Christmas reunion. Then they can take the shirts home as a keepsake. Choose a humorous family slogan or have somebody artistic make a sketch of a special house or other favorite spot.

As a show of solidarity, perhaps the kids could design a family flag to fly in the yard and at future family gatherings. Use crayons on cloth or make small paper versions and attach these to toothpicks as favors on the Christmas Day reunion dinner table. Symbols can be drawn that represent your family's interests. Is the name Gardner? Design flowers. Are you religious? Draw a Bible and cross. Is everyone crazy about spaghetti? How about drawing a bowlful? For other good ideas, send for "Gathering the Generations," a guide to family reunions (free from Better Homes and Gardens Family Network, Box 10237, Dept. M, Des Moines, IA 50336), or check local bookstores for other books.

*Bonus Idea 2:* Coming home for Christmas will cost much more for larger families, but holiday separations mean there is a vacuum in the heart, a small sad feeling that will not go away because someone is missing. Making it possible for folks to be together could mean more than money spent on gifts. Could you and your husband save all year to make it possible for all four of your married children and their families to be together on Christmas morning? Would everybody covenant together to put away twenty dollars a week per family so there could be a reunion in your hometown during the holidays next year? Maybe your accountant brother-in-law would agree to serve as treasurer, so money could be sent monthly to him to be put in an interest-bearing account. By the end of the year, the fund might hold enough to cover the high cost of togetherness for brothers and sisters, a beloved distant cousin, or an elderly aunt who struggles along on Social Security checks. If the plan works, and everyone wants to try it again, family members can take turns hosting so nobody has the burden over and over.

FOUR

Christmas Day

It is Christmas, and there are presents to be opened! When the new and glorious morn breaks, you may as well join the enthusiasm of young children jumping on your bed or climbing on your chest with glad tidings of great joy, for there is no rest after the crack of dawn for merry gentlemen and their wives.

If your children are a little older, however, and not even a mouse stirs early, maybe you can choose a happy way to wake everybody. Got a budding singer or trumpeter in the family? How about a rendition of "Joy to the World" from the top of the stairs? Or choose somebody to play beautiful Christmas music on the stereo in the hall. In our house, I recruited whomever I could from their beds to follow me from door to door singing "It's Beginning to Look a Lot Like Christmas." Everybody roused from sleep, then joined the noisy parade as we went through the house toward the tree (even Prince, the dog, and Kitty joined in). It is always appropriate to ask the younger children what special signal to use for waking up the older sleepyheads. They will be delighted to tinkle a bell or pull the stopper on the alarm clock so it goes off outside each person's bedroom door. If you have teenagers, ask one of them to get a cozy fire going in the fireplace before gifts are opened.

Early Christmas Morning

Just for fun, try one of these ideas. Once, we placed a huge "No Entrance until 9 A.M." sign on the door of the room where the tree and presents were ready. This allowed everyone's anticipation to build. Dad created extra fun by placing a tumble-down barricade of cardboard paper towel rolls, empty round potato chip containers, and soft plastic storage boxes inside a big trash bag above the door just in case somebody decided to sneak in. We

watched the minutes pass (ever so slowly!) on the kitchen clock as we ate our bacon and eggs. The whole family jokingly laughed together about the imaginary "Curse of the Punctured Pumpkin" that our teenager said would befall the unfortunate one who went in ahead of time (and, of course, somebody did!).

Another idea is to assign somebody to take pictures of the smaller children (or even sleepy-eyed parents) climbing out of bed, or of Grandmother wading through knee-deep package wrappings trying to fold them neatly for next year. Use a Polaroid camera so everybody can giggle over the photos right away.

Breakfast Specials

Does anybody take time to have breakfast on Christmas morning? If you are weary of watching the kids tear boxes open without really appreciating what is in them, slow things down by planning a sit-down breakfast an hour before the time to open gifts. Two small wrapped packages beside each plate can be opened before the meal. This may provide a calmer way to begin a frantic day.

To help small children get a good breakfast before the excitement begins, allow them to peek into their Christmas stockings as soon as they get up. Have goodies such as "the world's largest" banana or orange, small wrapped packages of cereal and a box of milk (found on most grocer's shelves), a mini can of fruit juice, a wrapped sweet roll, and maybe a candy cane or chocolate Santa for dessert tucked inside.

Bonus Idea 1: Create your own Christmas morning breakfast tradition, and give your family a feeling of unity and

love. Set out cereal and toast for starters, then place a little bowl of strawberries and cream at each plate. When each person is down to the last four berries, ask him or her to share something special about Christmas before eating each berry. Or ask each person for an affirmation of what Christ has meant in his or her life. After the meal, read together the Bible story of Jesus' birth.

*Bonus Idea 2:* Make breakfast out of the ordinary by serving a particular menu only on Christmas morning, such as blueberry or strawberry pancakes with real maple syrup, Mexican hot chocolate (add a teaspoon of orange juice concentrate to each cup of hot chocolate and serve with a cinnamon stick), or piping-hot creamed dried beef over homemade biscuits. Top off Christmas breakfast with tapioca pudding and whipped cream or red raspberry shortcake. Or make a country-style breakfast the most festive meal on Christmas Day, instead of dinner. Youngsters will appreciate not being pulled away from new toys for a lengthy meal later.

(P.S. Grandparents probably miss the early morning excitement now that their own kids are grown. Perhaps Gram and Gramps would enjoy staying overnight on Christmas Eve so they can join in the fun with your young children the next day. Note to grandparents: You can make a big hit with kids and add to early morning festivities by bringing along a gift grab bag for all ages to enjoy just before or after breakfast.)

Countdown Santa

Hallelujah, the time has come! Relatives bearing gifts have traveled from afar, kids (adults, too) are brimming with excitement. A lot of creative energy has gone into locating that

"perfect" present that will bring delight into the recipient's eyes. Everybody is ready to tear into packages . . . but wait! Maybe gift opening can be a bit different this year.

1. Before the family gathers, assign a fun duty to each of the children. Watch the happy chatter when the flurry of activities gets underway as different children hurry to flip on tree lights, scoot here and there to distribute gifts in groups of five, collect discarded ribbons and bows, race to gather up used wrapping paper in trash bags, and help an elderly grandmother read tags and open her gifts.

2. Tell everybody that the family will take turns opening one gift at a time for the first five gifts. This will help stretch out the fun, and create an environment in which everyone can enjoy each other's presents. Sometimes in the normal gift-opening flurry, the name of the giver is lost or the sentiment of some gifts is not fully appreciated. Allow time for the giver to explain his or her choice. Did it take Sis four hundred hours to complete the counted cross-stitch piece for Mom? Did the kids use a new microwave recipe for making the fudge they gave to Dad? Perhaps you can open your gifts "by prescription," taking one every few hours. Spending time with kids and their new toys and opening gifts at intervals helps settle children down and helps everybody savor the season much more.

3. Call a halt to Christmas morning madness by saving the largest and most exciting gifts until five o'clock. Or spread gift-getting from Christmas morning to New Year's. Part of the fun will be rattling and poking the boxes and guessing about

contents every day. Small things that might have gone unappreciated will become a treat on December 28.

4. For more fun, consider having a family "Yuletide mouse" stir around on Christmas Eve to hide gifts in secret nooks and crannies that only mice know about. This idea is a winner for kids, especially if you stop everything on Christmas morning to watch the gift hunt. Or hide one "finders, keepers" gift in a closet, basement, or refrigerator. Then give clues and watch the scurrying!

5. Allow children to open gifts on Christmas morning at their own pace. There will be at least one showstopper that will put a hold on everything. If the youngster wants to try out new roller skates right then and there, why not? Why try to hurry on to other presents just because you want to see the expression on her face when she sees a new bike or because the family will be arriving for dinner soon? Put unopened gifts aside until the spurt of excitement subsides. If relatives have showered a baby with too many toys and he is overwhelmed, allow Baby to open each gift separately to please aunts and uncles, then put them away to get out one at a time later.

Fun Ideas for Christmas Afternoon

Nobody wants Christmas to be over at eight o'clock in the morning after gifts are opened, or even at two in the afternoon when everyone is patting stuffed stomachs. So use one or two of these well-planned afternoon activities for stretching out your Christmas fun. They may even become next year's traditions.

1. One year after dinner, when we were all too sleepy to move and conversation ran slow (as it always did), I got out the big box where I had dropped photos for years. I sat at the dining-room table, complete with photos and the new album I had bought, and started sorting. It wasn't long before aunts, uncles, cousins, and my own children gathered around. Soon we were having a wonderful time, joking and laughing as we sorted, passing pictures around and reminiscing. We all remarked how easy it is to forget the good times. Soon the snapshots were laying in neat, family-by-family piles. Some were even arranged neatly in the album. Now photo time and old family movie time have become a regular part of our Christmas afternoon. My children and grandchildren adore hooting and hollering at their parents' antics on old films.

   In your house this year, maybe Great-grandmother could bring along an ancient album containing tintypes that were passed on by her parents. Or you could have everyone bring photos and albums for a fun time of sharing and remembering. Give it a try!

2. Look over games given to the children, and invite folks to play some of them. How about a game of dominoes or Monopoly or Trivial Pursuit? After awhile, one or two folks will emerge as champs to challenge others. The good-natured spirit of competition can be a lot of fun.

3. Make a long-distance phone call to a faraway relative, letting everyone talk a little. Each person should jot down a few newsy personal items ahead of time so the recipient will not hear the same message from everyone. Or arrange with the telephone company to set up a family conference call so that

all distant and nearby family members can join on one line at the same time from their homes. (Note: Check out the cost ahead of time to avoid a post-Christmas shock.)

4. Ask a family member to tape casual conversation at the dinner table, as well as a Christmas Day message from each guest, to be sent to someone who could not attend. Better yet, Dad can make a family video production to capture the children's excitement as they open gifts, cousin Alvin gnawing on a drumstick, or the family singing carols with Mom at the electronic keyboard. Your local audio-video store can make copies of these wonderful memories to send as late gifts or to keep in touch across the miles with far-flung relatives.

Bonus Idea: If a loved one is missing from the holiday dinner table, prepare a "Christmas Day Memory Book." Assign everyone a blank page to fill. Dad could take Polaroid pictures. Your ten-year-old daughter could write a letter describing Aunt Toty's charming new husband and the world's best mincemeat pie, which she has just eaten. A teenager can interview an older relative and write down her cheery greetings. Let Uncle Don describe the woodworking plans for his new bandsaw, and ask Sis to keep a log of the best and funniest gifts received. The distant one will adore being part of your Christmas and the book may just become an heirloom.

5. St. Francis of Assisi once said, "If I knew the Emperor, I would ask him to proclaim that on Christmas Day everyone should throw out food for the birds, and those who had beasts in the stable should give them especially good fod-

der, for love of the child Jesus born in a manger." Some Slavic people still celebrate the Feast of Stephen, on December 26, with this custom of sharing Christmas with wildlife.

Why not give this a try? Spend part of Christmas afternoon decorating an outside tree with snacks for feathered friends. Have a supply of bird seed, small net sachets of suet, apple pieces, bread cubes, and unshelled peanuts on hand. Have children gather pinecones to be spread with peanut butter or string garlands of raisins, cranberries, and popcorn. If you put out thistle and sunflower seeds, different birds, such as finches and cardinals, are more likely to join the fun. Most birds go searching for a meal in the late afternoon, so have your offering out by then.

6. After dinner, invite anybody who wants to come to join you in a stroll down the road to walk off a few calories, or to get a bit of fresh air and a change of scenery. You probably will be surprised at the number of takers. Talking while walking together gives people an opportunity to share good conversation and catch up on news. It helps close generation gaps, too.

7. Use Christmas dinner to reach out to others. Suggest that each guest bring along a toy, clothing, canned meat, or some other nonperishable treat to place in a box by your front door. Later you can all go to deliver the box to the downtown soup kitchen or to a children's home or mission house.

Bonus Idea 1: Have each family that brings a prepared dish fix a smaller, "extra" amount in a disposable covered container. While preparations for the big dinner are under way, or

when things quiet down afterward, Aunt Sue and the kids can take the delicious dishes to someone who will appreciate them. Do you know a young wheelchair-bound woman whose mom has full responsibility for all home duties and care? Could you deliver Christmas dinner down the street to a home where the family is facing some difficulty? Such recipients probably will appreciate being relieved of the need to spend the day preparing food and will enjoy being able to spend more time with their families. (If you follow this idea, be sure all recipients know ahead of time what you are doing.)

*Bonus Idea 2:* Assign everybody a name, then ask them to prepare a "wish" card for that person, which they will then read aloud after dinner. For example: "Today I wish for you healing from your arthritis pain and much love and peace in your heart." Most folks feel good doing these kinds of things, but it takes someone to initiate the idea and carry it out. Why not you?

8. To keep your kids from pigging out, share sweets with others right after Christmas. Gather up surplus wrapped peppermints and boxes of ribbon candy to take to a local nursing home on Christmas afternoon. Or hang candy canes on a little clothesline strung between a couple of trees in your front yard, next to the sidewalk. The neighborhood youngsters will likely grab them up on the way home after their first day back at school. Sharing your sweet treats will extend Christmas right on into January.

9. What is Christmas without a holiday "spread"? It is easy to make your own tablecloth to pass on to future generations. To cover the table, use several yards of plain red, green, or

ecru fabric. Or use a plain, colored, flat bed sheet. Fray the ends for an easy fringe and have embroidery thread, needles, and scissors on hand. When dinner dishes and food are cleared, invite everyone to draw a personal message on the cloth with a soft lead pencil or to trace a child's hand or a baby's foot. Let cousin Jim, who loves tennis, sketch a tennis racket and sign his name inside it. Outline a blue ribbon for Grandma because her much-loved coconut cakes win first prize at the county fair nearly every year. Ask everyone to embroider their own design, or maybe ask the eldest person or someone who loves sewing to take the spread home to complete the designs in her most exquisite embroidery stitches. Just be sure it is ready for dinner next Christmas.

Each year, ask for new additions to the cloth. You will soon find guests comparing memories and teens seeking out the handprints they made when they were tiny tots. Pass the tablecloth from hostess to hostess for holiday meals in years ahead.

10. Calendar tampering: Delay the family holiday dinner until December 26. Children will have more hours to enjoy toys and other gifts at home on Christmas Day, and adults will have plenty of time to show youngsters how to play new games and to put together gift bicycles, wagons, and robots. What greater disappointment can there be for a child than to be turned away with "Wait until tomorrow" when he or she presents a new toy for assembly on Christmas Day? Also, students and others coming home can travel cheaper and easier on the day after Christmas.

Making Christmas Day Mean More

Do you want to change the focus of the day from receiving gifts to setting a day apart to honor Christ? Do you feel uneasy about suggesting the turnaround? Often, all it takes is someone like you to initiate new ideas. You may be surprised at the willingness of a crotchety old uncle to join in singing carols or to hold hands as the family prays. Family members could be silently yearning for more closeness with God and others. Maybe some of these ideas could work for you and your family.

1. Invite guests to come early so they can go to church with you on Christmas morning. If your church does not have a service, find one that does. Many liturgical churches emphasize Christmas worship. Even the children will likely enjoy the beauty of the sanctuary and the worship experience, especially if there is a Little Cherub's choir or an orchestra.

2. Ask a family member to lead in a prayer of thanksgiving before eating Christmas dinner, or repeat the Lord's Prayer aloud together, or suggest singing a familiar hymn like "Blest Be the Tie That Binds" or "Joy to the World." In our family, we invited our children to compose the holiday table prayer. Ten-year-old Gale's was something like, "Lord, thank you for Jesus because he cleared the way to make us clean so we could come right close to you in prayer to talk to you and ask for things we need." Her older sister prayed, "Help us to love each other as much as you loved the world by sending your Son. Thank you for food, too. Amen."

3. A Tennessee wife says that her family forms a circle around the Christmas dinner table, each offering a sentence prayer

thanking God for one good thing that has come into their lives since the last time they were together. "Even children can come up with one sentence, so nobody is embarrassed," she notes. If there is a particular crisis in your family, unite before God in prayer. Supporting each other in prayer helps everyone to develop strong empathy and concern for needs and problems. Family gatherings are an appropriate time to build this kind of mutual caring, a caring that Jesus taught.

4. Announce at the Christmas dinner table that you would like everyone to be thinking about an interesting story of a past Christmas. Explain that you will share your stories later, while eating fruitcake or plum pudding by candlelight. Suggest that stories can be silly, sad, sentimental, or enlightening. Older people will especially enjoy sharing from their richest past Christmases. Some in the family will likely recall times when they felt especially close to God or will share what the heavenly Father has been doing in their lives to bless them. After those accustomed to talking about God tell their experiences, the others will realize that they, too, have had such times and may gain courage to share them.

A military wife said, "Three years ago, I requested that each guest jot down on paper at least one tradition or change they would like to see adopted in future years to make Christmas more fun and especially to reflect more of the true meaning. Then I read the ideas aloud and we discussed them. No one objected when our newlywed daughter suggested we try several religious activities. Even my not-very-churchy cousin's family seemed willing. It was as if each person

yearned privately for more of God in our celebration, but nobody wanted to be first to suggest change. Next year? A cousin who has begun attending church for the first time in his life has volunteered to lead Christmas table prayers, and Uncle Bob will read a Psalm. It is a nice way for all of us to be growing together."

5. Hand unlit candles to everybody at the table after Christmas dinner. The host or hostess can move around the circle, lighting everybody's candle one-by-one, then touching each one on the shoulder with a specific wish. "James, I wish for you a job that you will love." "Teresa, my prayer for you is for a new and loving friend to take the place of your beloved neighbor who died last month." These wish-prayers can be prepared ahead by the host. As the family grows more comfortable with the candle ritual, all of the wishes could turn into short prayers or even into a Christmas worship.

Great Ideas for Busy Christmas Cooks

These days, Grandma might hold down a full-time job and need all the help she can get to put Christmas dinner on the table. Here are some ways to get the cook out of the kitchen faster. Perhaps some year you could honor the faithful cook at a Christmas dinner party in a local restaurant. Schedule ahead! Many eating places are closed on the holiday. Or you could have dinner brought into Grandma's house by a caterer.

1. Borrow an idea from today's restaurants and serve buffet style. Yes, even on Christmas! Letting guests help themselves in the kitchen makes them feel much more at home,

too. Borrow card tables from friends or folding chairs and tables from the church or club so guests can seat themselves randomly once plates are filled. Tray tables can be provided for the overflow crowd in the living room. Kids and many adults enjoy sitting crosslegged on the floor, especially if you provide a cozy fire in the fireplace. Children might enjoy eating together in one of the youngsters' rooms. Keep in mind that it is the good food and the company of relatives and friends that count.

2. Five-star idea: Make Christmas dinner easy by freezing turkey, gravy, dressing, cranberries, and other leftovers from Thanksgiving. Instead of being a menu problem, these food items become a delicious and easy Christmas meal by simply adding soups, cheese, or a salad.

3. "Prepare a duty roster," says a Georgia woman who often felt overwhelmed on Christmas Day by too many visitors roaming around her kitchen and spurts of help (and non-help) being offered as she prepared dinner. "I decided that if folks were going to hang around waiting to eat, I would get them organized," she says. This lady lists every guest's name and assigns chores such as washing fresh veggies, carrying in chairs, carving the turkey, setting the table, doing dishes, making gravy, mashing potatoes, or taking young children for a walk to get them out from underfoot. Each task must be completed by two o'clock, which is sit-down time at the table. The first thing folks do when they come in the front door is to check the duty roster hung in the front hall to see which task is theirs. "There is lots of joking and friendly jostling for a place at the kitchen counter as each pitches in to help, the woman says, "and every-

body seems to have a good time. My children love to call me
'The Dictator' (always with a friendly twinkle in the eye), but
all the jobs get done. Their work relieves me of trivial tasks
and gives me unpressured time to complete last-minute preparations that only the hostess can do."

FIVE

The Family at New Year's

New Year's is a time to assess the past, then look ahead and begin again. A family can thank God for times when they have lived up to their own expectations and dream new dreams when they have not. Planning together, even informally, for the upcoming months adds a new dimension of expectation to days ahead. Here are the ideas that others have used successfully to enhance family togetherness and extend the spirit of Christmas into the new year.

Looking Back

On New Year's Eve, create an atmosphere of togetherness by abolishing bedtime rules and having a treat. Plan a pizza supper for the family, and serve it in front of the fireplace or in the living room about eleven o'clock. If you don't want to fix a whole meal, brew hot spiced cider and have the teens make popcorn balls as everyone gathers to talk about events of the past year. Spark the discussion by asking:

1. What has been the high point of the year for our family?

2. What is the best thing our family did together this year? The worst?

3. What is the best thing that happened to you personally? The worst?

4. What is your biggest disappointment?

5. How have you changed?

6. Who was the most important person in your life this last year? Why?

7. What is one thing you wish you had done differently?

8. What are you most thankful for right now?

Encourage gratitude for things everyone tends to take for granted such as music, eyesight, hearing, or Christmas trees and cranberries, or eggs and toast for breakfast.

My family laughed together as we remembered four rained-out camping trips, and we cried a little as we reminisced about our beloved Kitty who died in September. This kind of sharing stirs the warmest of memories and brings a family close together. At midnight, bring in the new year by holding hands and saying the Lord's Prayer aloud.

Bonus Idea 1: Maybe Mom or Big Sister can be enlisted to begin a family diary to record small and large happenings, celebrations, personal thoughts, opinions overheard, and changes around home. Then read the accounts when the family gathers next New Year's. The writing will likely stir a good time of conversation when forgotten events are brought up.

Bonus Idea 2: Try this idea from Karen Yoder:

> Two years ago we did something on New Year's Eve that appears destined to become a family tradition. We used a checklist of mental capabilities (such as "I can tie my shoelaces," and "I can identify five trees") which we helped our two oldest (who were then ages seven and five) to complete. We also used a long strip of paper (like adding machine tape) to record each family member's height.
>
> We placed these things in a time capsule (a large brown envelope) and saved them for a year. It is hard to describe

the fun and joy we had the second New Year's Eve, first filling out the checklists, and then comparing them to the previous year's. We remeasured everyone; the change in the children was quite staggering (more graphic than in health records!). The children also included drawings on their checklists.

Some of the other questions on our checklist, based on a list we found in a devotional publication, were: "I can multiply by threes," and "I can sew on a button," and "I can name the president and vice-president of the United States." Stories and poems, along with the drawings, would be great. I added a few philosophical comments. The idea behind it is to see how our perspective and feelings (and, for growing artists, ability) *do change*—even that of the "old folks." When we were done, we replaced everything in the time capsule. We eagerly await New Year's Eve this year.*

Bonus Idea 3: Looking for solutions to broken resolutions? On New Year's Eve, ask everybody to take pen and paper around midnight and privately write down resolutions for the coming year. Have adults and older children help the little ones. Mostly, they will be things each person plans to do better (lose ten pounds, eat less cholesterol and meat and more fiber, keep boasting or hot tempers under better control, or stop procrastinating and be on time). There will be some lighter promises, too, especially from teens (such as diving off the diving board by next summer, reading a classic such as *Jane Eyre,* paying a brother bor-

*Reprinted with permission from Resource Publications, Inc., 160 E. Virginia St., Suite 290, San Jose, CA 95112.

rowed money, or sampling every luscious dessert in the local cafeteria). Have each person seal the written resolutions in an envelope that is labeled with his or her name. Then put the envelopes away to be pulled out next New Year's. Next year, you will most likely feel a wonderful element of intrigue and mystery just before opening the envelopes and reading last year's hopes and dreams aloud. There will also probably be lots of laughs and hugs when some dreams have been fulfilled (like Maria's pledge to become engaged). When disappointments or disillusionments are reviewed, affirm each other and remind everybody that life starts over, in a sense, at the beginning of every new year.

Bonus Idea 4: Have a "New Year's Is for Caring" ceremony. After gathering to light the tree for the last time, allow each person to open one Christmas present, which they have saved for this night. Next, have everyone sit down around the tree to give appreciation gifts to each other. Take turns giving thanks in Christ's name for the gift of some specific character quality or for some good deed done this year. For example:

To a teen brother: I am thankful that you haven't argued so much with Dad lately about getting home on time when you go out. You seem more loving and willing to cooperate. Since Mom is not feeling very well, the quieter atmosphere around here makes our home more peaceful, and I think we all need that.

To Mom: I especially appreciate your cheerfulness and hopefulness when I share my problems with you.

To Dad: I know you always want the best for all of us. Thanks for your encouragement and support.

Everybody enjoys receiving affirmation. There is likely to be much excited whispering, especially among the children as they

try to guess what others will think about their words of appreciation. Just watch the happiness reflected in the eyes of old and young alike as they anticipate what good things will be said of them. Sometimes these words will be spoken with a lump in the throat, but when it is all over, the evening just may turn out to be the best and longest remembered part of the Christmas season.

Down Comes the Tree

It is no secret that almost everybody will eagerly join in helping to set up the Christmas tree. When it comes to taking the tree down, however, helpers somehow disappear. This can be a melancholy matter. In our house, nobody ever volunteered to help dismantle our elegant Norfolk pine or pack away the tree trimmings. One mom, however, gently prods willing attitudes from her family by placing a small gold foil-wrapped gift for each person among the branches of the tree as soon as it is put up. The children know that the little boxes can be opened only after the last decorations are removed and the ornaments put away neatly in boxes. Your children may enjoy the idea of more gifts so much that they will beg to take down the tree before New Year's Day. Now wouldn't that be a pleasant state of Yuletide affairs? The tiny presents can be inexpensive things, such as a mini-flashlight, a ball, a game of jacks, or packets of bubble gum. Choose anything that seems just right to prime willing spirits and keep the happy glow of Christmas alive longer.

Another idea is to hang individual boxes of luscious chocolates or a wrapped chocolate Santa for each helper, which are not to be eaten until the family begins removing decorations on January 1. No treats for lazy louts! My friend's grandmother invites the fam-

ily over to help take down her tree, and she gives each helper a specially selected ornament to take home.

*Bonus Idea 1:* Creativity spoken here! One family waits until about seven o'clock in the evening on New Year's to take down the tree. They cut it up and use the wood to make a glowing fire, then sit around it and enjoy a chili supper. The gingerbread house that Mom always makes for the holidays is unwrapped from cellophane and eaten as dessert.

When we lived in New Hampshire, our eight-year-old suggested an outdoor weenie roast. So we all bundled up in jackets, mittens, and scarves and roasted hot dogs and marshmallows on the backyard grill (in thirty-degree weather!). The night before, ice had formed on the street out front, so we dug out our skates and had great fun twirling, twisting, and tumbling by moonlight (reinforced by our front porch light).

Bonus Idea 2: One handyman-grandfather sometimes uses carpenter's tools and whittling knives to make his family's Christmas tree into something memorable, such as bookends, carved figurines, or a plaque to give as a gift next year. He delights in carving his name and the year on the base of each piece, so future generations can know and remember the origin of the gift.

Bonus Idea 3: Christmas can continue to be a focal point of family celebration during Lent and Easter time, if someone is willing to make a cross from the trunk of the tree. During Lent, you can place the Christmas tree cross on the kitchen table, in a

*Reprinted by permission from Resource Publications, Inc., 160 E. Virginia St. Suite 290, San Jose, CA 95112.

family prayer corner, or wherever the family gathers for celebrations. When Easter morning arrives, drape it with a piece of white fabric as a proclamation that "Christ is risen!"

To make a cross, follow these instructions from Resource publications.*

Things you will need:
1. Your used Christmas tree

2. Small saw

3. Very sharp knife

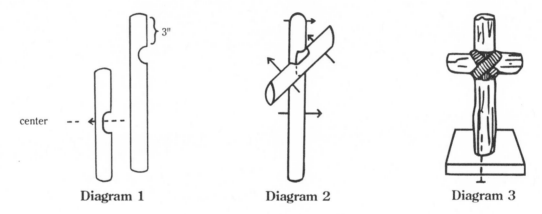

4. Twelve-inch piece of half-inch-wide grosgrain ribbon

5. Sandpaper

6. Block of scrap wood, approximately six-by-six inches wide and half an inch thick. (This can be obtained from a neighborhood hardware store or lumber yard.)

7. Large flathead nail and hammer.

How to proceed:

1. Cut two small "logs" from the lower end of the Christmas tree trunk. One log should be about twelve inches long and the other about eight inches long. (It may be necessary to remove lower branches to get logs this length.)

2. Measure three inches down from the top of the longer log and cut a notch in the wood with a sharp knife. The notch should be as wide as the cross log and half as deep as the log being cut. (See diagram 1.)

3. Cut a similar notch in the very center of the shorter log.

4. Fit notched logs together. (See diagram 2.)

5. Wind purple ribbon around log joinings and tuck ends in. This will decorate and reinforce the joinings.

6. Sand lower end of cross so that it fits flush against the flat piece of wood.

7. Using a large, flathead nail, join cross to base by nailing through base center up into the center of the log. (See diagram 3.)

More Ideas for New Year's Day

1. Spend January 1 getting rid of the old to make room for the new. Clean out closets and discard unneeded items, catch up on that long list of chores, make long-delayed phone calls at low holiday rates, balance the checkbook, make a needed

apology, take a second look at greeting cards, keep your promise to play a game of Monopoly with your seven-year-old, clean out the fireplace, or put workbench or sewing machine drawers or a guest bedroom in order. As you and your family put the old behind and make way for whatever lies ahead, the new year with its clean slate (and clean cupboards or drawers) will come alive with promise for a fresh and exciting start.

2. Get the whole family hooked on gratefulness. New Year's is a good time to gather everybody at the dining room table to write Christmas thank-you notes. Have several boxes of handsome or absurd or cute stationery on hand. Adults and teens will need to write thank-you's for small youngsters, but let little ones enclose a drawing showing how they use the gift. Children will enjoy sticking on stamps and going with you to the mailbox, too. Have a plate of cookies nearby for everyone to enjoy when the letters are completed. This all will help children realize early on that expressing gratefulness is important and even fun.

One mother, who finds it difficult to get her sons to write thank-yous, tucks their Christmas stockings with a box of pretty stationery, a book of stamps, and a pretty little notebook so they can list names of each gift's donor. Later, she goes through and writes in addresses for them.

Continuing the Celebration: Epiphany

Though we often yearn to have the holiday spirit last, we seem to get over Christmas all too quickly once the gifts are unwrapped and the turkey tidbits are made up into casseroles. Some folks, however, continue the celebration until January 6, for that is when Epiphany is observed. Epiphany is a church festival commemorating the arrival of the wise men at the birthplace of Jesus. In some countries, it is called the Eve of Kings, and the best gifts and the biggest feast are reserved for Epiphany Eve.

Even if your particular church does not make a practice of observing this festival, perhaps your family would enjoy reading together why others celebrate this joyous day, both at home and in special worship services. Consider extending the religious emphasis of Christmas over into January. Ask your pastor for more information about Epiphany, or spend a few minutes in your public or church library to locate books with suggested short family activities.

SIX

Coping with Christmas

Resource ideas for happily
surviving the holidays

Sometimes during December, *nothing* seems calm, *nothing* seems bright, and there are no silent nights.

We remember Christmases past, the tumult of joys, the wondrous smells and delicious tastes, and the visions of sugarplums that danced in our heads. We recall the beloved people who made the season warm and loving. We want our own celebrations to be just like the ones we used to know. Somehow, though, we do not quite know how to make our celebrations come out the way we want them to. In days gone by, when we were not responsible for the outcome, everyone seemed to sail right through the holidays with smiles and happiness. Generally, we don't recall relatives who did not get along, terrifying traffic jams at the airport or bus station, struggles behind the scenes in the kitchen, whiny children, harried adults working under deadlines, the hassle of baking and cooking and shopping, dizzying spending, or Aunt Mame's Christmas blues. How did it all happen so wonderfully? How did Grandma and Auntie keep the peace of Christmas and still take on the responsibility of planning it all for the family? Though we can't return to that seemingly simpler era, there are things we can do to ease the holiday stress.

This chapter offers resources with "uncommon good sense" for surviving Christmas. Included are a fill-in budget checklist to help get a handle on where your money really goes, ideas about how to get cash for the Christmas crunch, and tips for cutting gift lists and stretching time and dollars. Also included are several how-to sections—all of which will help you create the holiday you really want.

How Not to Go Broke This Christmas

Busted budgets make folks yearn for a simpler celebration. Christmas catalogs from famous department stores unashamedly suggest five-thousand-dollar crystal pieces, and a New York wine shop offers champagne-flavored toothpaste at $19.50 for two tubes. But many of us enter the season worrying about bank accounts and checkbooks that already are in disarray from daily family demands. We wonder how to keep our heads above water with the added December financial stress, or we recall ugly arguments last January with sad children looking on, when bills piled up and tempers flared. We vow to do better—but how?

Just because you are pinching pennies does not mean you have to settle for a lackluster Christmas. What it does mean is that you must make the effort to limit spending and to do so wisely. One thing you definitely need is a detailed and specific budget. This budget must cover *everything*. There must be a firm limit on total amount spent. Sure, budgets are made to be broken, but getting yours on paper will help bring impossible expectations down to earth. Keeping a close tally of expenses as December rolls along will give you and your family added incentive to reign in unnecessary spending. You will get a better feel for what is important and what isn't—and it will help you check January bills for accuracy.

Following is a suggested family budget. Consider it carefully, then streamline it to fit your specific needs (See pages 160–162)

Fill in and then total up estimated costs of everything. Most folks greatly underestimate the cost of small items. Did you? Does the total in column one match your budget? If not, plan to cut back purchases and rearrange figures so they fit your pocketbook. Cancel the word "cheapskate" every time it comes to mind and replace it with "wise common sense." Your aim is to have as

warm and wonderful a Christmas as possible while avoiding a vicious January where you are digging out from under a pile of bills. Christmas was never meant to leave celebrators crushed financially. What would Jesus think if he came by and saw it happening? When you center more activity around the real meaning of the holiday you will help budgeting take on a more sensible view. Enjoy the challenge!

How to Stretch Gift-Giving Dollars

What begins as an inexpensive custom sometimes blossoms into a burden. When brother Tom and wife, Ellie, were first married, it was easier to exchange gifts. Now, however, they have four children. The decision to continue such traditions must be balanced against cost. Budget cuts may mean you need to celebrate a bit differently, but habits are hard to break and it may take a family powwow to move in new directions. Maybe you can "make cents" by suggesting one of these cost-cutting ideas to your family. If you desire to make a more financially sensible Christmas, it's a pretty sure bet that they do, too.

1. Draw names to give a gift to one, not all family members. Have each person write his or her name on a file card along with several gift suggestions. Everyone will end up happy with their present, but the surprise element remains.

2. Ask the whole family to set a price limit on gifts and stick to it. Agree on the amount in advance, and insist on cooperation from everyone. Or cut back on the amount *you* spend on each gift, paying no attention to others. Double-check the figure and make a covenant with yourself not to exceed your set limit. Make it work!

Family Christmas Budget

This complete budget outlines nearly every possible Christmas expenditure. No family will have all of these expenses, of course, but there will probably be many more incidentals than you expected. Fill in realistic estimates or write in what you spent last year. If you are uncertain, use the highest figure. Things cost a lot these days! When you have written an estimate for each item in column one, total everything on the last page. Then compare the entire cost with the amount you have on hand. To help yourself plan for next year, be sure to fill in this year's amounts, either as you actually spend them or very soon after the holidays.

19__ Budgeted Amount $_____

	Estimated Cost	Amount Actually Spent

GIFTS

Gifts for family and friends

	Estimated Cost	Amount Actually Spent
1. _____	_____	_____
2. _____	_____	_____
3. _____	_____	_____
4. _____	_____	_____
5. _____	_____	_____
6. _____	_____	_____
7. _____	_____	_____

Special gifts for others (postman, boss, newspaper carrier)

1. _____	_____	_____
2. _____	_____	_____

	Estimated Cost	Amount Actually Spent
3. _____	_____	_____
4. _____	_____	_____
5. _____	_____	_____

Gift wrapping

Wrapping paper, tissue, brown paper for mailing	_____	_____
Ribbon, bows, tags	_____	_____
Scotch tape, masking, strapping tape	_____	_____
Special mailing boxes, cartons, tubes, padded envelopes	_____	_____
Professional gift wrapping (about $3 per package)	_____	_____

Charities and church donations

1. _____	_____	_____
2. _____	_____	_____
3. _____	_____	_____

POSTAGE AND FREIGHT

Postage for sending newsletter	_____	_____

Freight costs for sending packages

1. _____	_____	_____
2. _____	_____	_____
3. _____	_____	_____
4. _____	_____	_____

Overseas postage and freight

1. _____	_____	_____
2. _____	_____	_____
3. _____	_____	_____
4. _____	_____	_____
5. _____	_____	_____

CHRISTMAS CARDS AND LETTERS

Store bought cards	_____	_____

160

	Estimated Cost	Amount Actually Spent
Materials to make Christmas cards	_____	_____
Printing or copying of newsletter	_____	_____
Envelopes	_____	_____
Photographs for inserts	_____	_____
Seals or stickers	_____	_____

DECORATING

	Estimated Cost	Amount Actually Spent
Christmas tree and stand	_____	_____
Light replacement sets and extra bulbs	_____	_____
Tree ornaments or craft books; materials to make ornaments	_____	_____
Table centerpiece	_____	_____
Outdoor decorations	_____	_____
Miscellaneous (candles, wreaths, garlands, flowers, crèche, Advent items)	_____	_____

FOOD

	Estimated Cost	Amount Actually Spent
Christmas dinner ingredients	_____	_____
Christmas Eve food	_____	_____
Special hostess food (eggnog, punch, nuts, snack foods)	_____	_____
Baking ingredients for cookies, cakes	_____	_____
New kitchen equipment (cookie cutters, food processor, food molds)	_____	_____
Food for potluck suppers at church	_____	_____
Paper plates, cups, napkins	_____	_____
Special liners (tablecloths, placemats)	_____	_____
Convenience or restaurant food for the family to relieve the cook of kitchen duties during the busy season	_____	_____

TRAVEL

Local travel for shopping, attending events

	Estimated Cost	Amount Actually Spent
Gasoline	_____	_____
Bus, subway fares, taxi	_____	_____

Long distance travel

	Estimated Cost	Amount Actually Spent
Airline, train, or bus tickets, gasoline	_____	_____
Meals on the road	_____	_____
Lodging	_____	_____
Miscellaneous (maps, disposable diapers, pet boarding, luggage purchase, car maintenance, rental car, house gifts, souvenirs, parking and toll fees)	_____	_____

ENTERTAINING

Food, beverages, or catering

	Estimated Cost	Amount Actually Spent
1. Function #1:	_____	_____
2. Function #2:	_____	_____
3. Function #3:	_____	_____

Invitations, postage

	Estimated Cost	Amount Actually Spent
1. Function #1:	_____	_____
2. Function #2:	_____	_____
3. Function #3:	_____	_____

Other

	Estimated Cost	Amount Actually Spent
Decorations	_____	_____
Special serving pieces to be purchased	_____	_____
Hostess gifts	_____	_____
Rental of formal clothing	_____	_____
Purchase of party clothes	_____	_____

	Estimated Cost	Amount Actually Spent

Babysitting
____(number of times) x $____(cost of
each) = $____ (total)

HOUSEGUESTS

____(number of times) x $____(cost per
day) = $____(total)

	Estimated Cost	Amount Actually Spent
Eating out, tips	_____	_____
New linens (sheets, blankets, towels)	_____	_____
Higher utility bills	_____	_____

Entertainment of guests

Museum, movie, concert tickets	_____	_____
Extra gasoline costs	_____	_____
Games, toys for visiting children	_____	_____
Home items (new furniture, curtains, slipcovers)	_____	_____

MISCELLANEOUS

Christmas catalogs	_____	_____

	Estimated Cost	Amount Actually Spent
Camera film, supplies, developing	_____	_____
Christmas records and tapes	_____	_____
Tickets for special holiday events	_____	_____
Wood for fireplace	_____	_____
Dry cleaning	_____	_____
New houseplants	_____	_____
Professional housecleaning, carpet cleaning	_____	_____
Redecorating	_____	_____
Home repairs	_____	_____
Long-distance phone calls	_____	_____
Haircuts	_____	_____
Advent and Christmas books	_____	_____

Totals

	Total Estimated Cost	Total Actually Spent
	$ _____	$_____

3. Give one gift to each household.

4. Spend time reviewing your gift list and cut out some names. Are you still having a box of live holly sent to your daughter-in-law's parents ten years after the wedding? Perhaps you can explain that you are simplifying your celebration and want to remember them in other ways. A pleasant phone call or a letter explaining what you're doing and why can be a start. It is quite likely that others will be relieved and admire your courage. Once the routine is broken, the likelihood of more meaningful gifts is increased, too.

5. If there are lots of kids on your gift list, select one of these ideas:

   - One year give gifts to children under eight years old; the next year, give to those nine years old and over.

   - Rotate giving to boys one year, girls the next.

   - Agree on gifts under five dollars for kids up to nine years old. After that, give family gifts like a game or picnic equipment for all to enjoy.

   - Give gifts to children only, eliminating adults on your list.

   - Suggest cutting out gift-giving to other people's children who are over a certain age, such as twelve or sixteen.

6. Encourage good budgeting for the children, too. Give them a certain amount of money to spend, making it clear that it must cover everybody. Kids learn to choose gifts carefully and will often spend an extraordinary amount of time and thought about each other's needs and desires.

7. Have everybody contribute one gift to a grab bag, setting a firm spending limit, which can be as little as a dollar. Each person, children included, gets to pull a present from the bag. Some families love the sheer silliness involved when Dad gets a pair of panty hose or Susie receives shaving cream. When such mismatched gifts are swapped among recipients, the giggling continues. Or you could have separate grab bags for children, men, and women.

8. Review your gift list to determine whether you might offer a gift of service for the person instead of buying a present. Stuck for ideas? How about promising to give a home perm, organize a carpool, or bring in an elderly neighbor's mail daily?

9. Tell the family that you specialize in birthday gifts. Then save the money and use it to celebrate your favorite people when their big day comes. Your present will likely be more appreciated then.

10. Suggest replacing expensive gift giving with the loving fellowship of a shared potluck holiday dinner for family and friends. The gratifying camaraderie will likely outdo the fleeting excitement of opening presents.

11. If you exchange gifts at work, initiate a low, low ceiling for amount spent on gifts. One small office group awards a "happy prize" to the worker who buys the most gift for the money (limit is two dollars). Some hobbyist-employee usually donates the prize, such as a hand-crocheted afghan, home-canned veggies, or a pair of handcrafted bookends. Another office group collects a dollar from each employee

to be given to a favorite charity instead of exchanging gifts. Other alternatives to suggest: have everybody kick in a small amount to make a really good eggnog punch that will serve as the focus of the office party; have everyone draw names and hand-make an appropriate gift for the other person.

12. Avoid gift-giving traps. Forget the guilt-wrapped present that you give only because you think you should. It will probably be too expensive and may be ill-chosen. Avoid "even-Steven" giving, too. Never mind trying to outguess what Aunt Jane's present will cost so you can match it. The numbers game can be unnerving and spoil the spirit of Christmas. So what if someone gave you a fifty-dollar check and you only bought socks for him? What really counts isn't the cost, it's whether or not you've put real thought and consideration into the gifts you give. Give what your heart and budget dictate. If a gift is too expensive for your pocketbook, don't buy it! Period.

Buying Tips That Will Save You Money

You can keep holiday expenses from skyrocketing and still not feel like Scrooge by considering some of these shrewd strategies before shelling out your hard-to-come-by dollars. To help stay financially solvent:

1. Shop early. Experts say that because selection is poorer and frustration levels higher, last-minute shoppers often end up buying far more expensive items than planned.

2. Search for gifts at good neighborhood garage and tag sales, flea markets, church bazaars, or in your own china cabinet, jewelry box, or cedar chest.

3. Purchase generic items bearing department or grocery store labels instead of brand names. Many items closely resemble those manufactured by a well-known company.

4. Determine ahead whether the item to be purchased will be used only occasionally or every day. Perhaps a less-expensive model or brand of food processor or juicer would do just as well.

5. Shop factory outlets, keeping in mind that you are buying the item, not the store's fashionable name.

6. To control impulse buying, shop with a list. Have in mind a designated amount to be spent on each person. Stick to the list regardless of whether you are shopping early or late. In general, the more expensive the gift, the more thought you should give to locating the best buy.

7. Purchase items that promise rebates. Watch magazine ads and department store bulletin boards for rebate coupons.

8. Watch for Christmas promotions—that's when stores often introduce new items at lower prices. Note also that things in low demand around the holidays, such as children's clothing or bed sheets, often are priced substantially lower in November and December. Consider these as gifts.

9. Almost everything goes on sale at one time or another. Set gift goals early in the year and shop sales all year round, beginning in January. Toys, Christmas cards, artificial trees, and items such as ribbon, yarn, fabric, and fake flowers often are 50 to 75 percent off the week after Christmas. Buying these to put away for use in twelve months will take a little determination, but may be worth it. In January, I like to buy up chocolate Santas, which I chop in the food processor and freeze for use as decorations for birthday cakes, cookies, puddings, and other desserts all year.

10. When ordering from stores such as Sears, Penney's, and Spiegel, ask for sale catalogs to see if the article you want is featured. Request toll-free numbers to call in orders. Picking up purchases yourself instead of having them sent to your home will save money, too.

11. Take advantage of sales on film for cameras. Watch for after-Christmas half-price or double print offers on developing. They are everywhere.

12. Instead of hiring department store service departments to wrap gifts, do it yourself and get the kids to help. Also, take advantage of free wrapping wherever available. Request free gift boxes and shopping bags, too!

13. Stay away from gourmet gift boxes of citrus, cheese, nuts, and smoked meat. Packing your own fruit baskets, or cookie or nut tins saves a lot of money.

14. Keep in mind that most specialty items advertised on television during the holidays are not offered at bargain prices. C.O.D. fees are very, very expensive, too.

15. Purchase a live Christmas tree when prices begin coming down, usually around December 18. Even the finest trees are often reduced 15 to 25 percent by then. Don't wait too long, though. Come December 24, savings may be greater, but you may have only leftover "twiggies" to choose from. Check prices to see if cutting your own tree at a local Christmas tree farm is cheaper. Or consider purchasing a live potted tree to plant later in the yard. One Georgia family saves money by trimming a beautiful floor plant with white bows and clear mini-lights instead of buying a tree.

16. Season the season with cards instead of gifts. Never mind the outrageously expensive boxes with velour Santas and gold filet edging. A 40 percent–off card with a well-chosen message from a discount store will do just as well. Someone figured out that the average cost of sending a card is over one dollar including postage, so review your list every few years and cut out those who get a gift and the ones you see often. Hand-deliver any cards you can. Or use holiday postcards, which cost less to buy and mail but still have plenty of room for a personal handwritten message.

Money-Saving Ideas Especially for the Family

1. Invite the family to celebrate Christmas later in December or on New Year's Day, or delay visiting friends until after December 25 so that you can take advantage of post-Christmas sales when buying gifts. Even almond bark and candied fruit will be marked down. On Christmas, give an I.O.U. with a picture of your gift clipped from a catalog; then purchase the wanted item at reduced prices the following week and deliver it then.

2. Ask the family to alternate homes for Christmas dinner so one household does not always bear the major food cost. Being in each other's homes makes folks feel closer, too.

3. Buy or make the same gift for everyone on your list. Purchasing in quantity can save both money and time. One family enjoys the togetherness of a project such as making candles from milk cartons or mixing up their grandmother's special white fruit cake recipe in big batches to give away.

4. Is your family's budget for holiday clothing tight? Buy or make one dress or suit for each to wear for all holiday dress-up occasions. Choose garments that are not so obviously Christmasy that they will be unsuitable any other time of year. It is not likely that the same crowd will attend the office Christmas party and the church banquet anyway—and even if they do, so what? Better yet, update last year's clothing by adding a wide sequined belt, lace collar and cuffs, matching jewelry, or (for Dad) a bright red vest. Share formal gowns and gold lamé

sweaters with a friend. For kids, steer away from little boys' velvet suits and little girls' lace dresses, no matter how adorable, because they may not be worn again soon and will be outgrown by next year.

Tips for Less-Expensive Entertaining

1. Simplify entertaining. Look through magazines and recipe books for ideas about inexpensive casseroles and decorations that might be just as good (or better!) than those you and your mom have always used. Ask the children to help prepare food instead of hiring a caterer, and remember that certain simple menus also allow the hostess more freedom. Serving lavish canapes and expensive liquors is really not essential to make guests feel at home. It is the warmth and caring of your hospitality that mean most.

Bonus Idea: Instead of bearing the full cost of entertaining, maybe you can locate a relative or friend to cohost a party so expenses (and preparation) can be shared.

2. Rent or borrow special kitchen equipment that you will use only once or twice. Ask friends about punch bowls, tablecloths, pasta machines, Bundt pans, and good china. Maybe you can also exchange baby-sitting with a good buddy.

Bonus Idea: Trim the trimmings! Using your ingenuity and creativity can cut costs of gift wrappings or decorations. If last year's gold glass balls were crushed in storage, trim the tree and gift packages with bows, candy canes, and homemade cookies or other goodies. Use greenery from the yard to dress up mantles

or tables or for making wreaths. Other available outdoor materials include pinecones, nuts, bunches of holly berries, dried flowers, and corn husks. If your yard has none of these, perhaps your neighbor will allow you to cut branches that he may need to prune back soon anyway.

Credit and Credit Cards

1. Never, never purchase an item just because payment terms are easy. Merchandise sold on "easier" terms is often marked up and sometimes comes with higher interest charges.

2. Avoid borrowing for Christmas. It is estimated that 30 percent of all credit card charges are made during the holidays. If you are tempted to buy something on time, figure out ahead how much interest you will pay. If you must charge, set a firm limit and take advantage of department store credit plans that allow you to pay for purchases in three monthly installments at no interest. To avoid overspending, envision how it feels to be inundated by January bills. Then imagine the joy of receiving bills totalling $00.00, or of paying your bills off early. To insure paying cold cash, one woman who is well aware of past credit card excesses froze all her credit cards in a bowl of ice during November and December. (Taking out a loan after the holidays to pay off charge card bills is foul play!)

3. If you decide to charge purchases, carry only one or at the most two credit cards while shopping so that you are not tricked into thinking that you're not spending much money

because the total on each card is quite low. Choose cards with no outstanding balance, and pay the bill during the twenty-five-day grace period before interest accrues. Stick a Post-It note to every card and keep a running tally of how much you are charging on each one.

Long-Distance Savings

1. Save postage money by selecting lightweight gifts that wrap easily and by mailing presents early so there is plenty of time for them to arrive without paying for costly next-day delivery (which can be about eighteen dollars for two pounds). Early mailing is especially important for overseas packages since boat rates for boxes are about one-fourth the cost of airmail. Take advantage of lower rates for books and printed matter both for overseas and in-country mailings. Compare U.S. Post Office costs with those of other delivery services, such as UPS or Federal Express. Ask for rate charts. Use brown paper grocery bags to wrap parcels instead of purchasing expensive rolls. Hand-deliver gifts to folks you see often. If you are flying to spend Christmas elsewhere, mail the gifts ahead. Never carry wrapped packages aboard; airport security guards may pull your beautiful wrappings apart to inspect.

2. Pack all family gifts into one box since parcel post rates get cheaper as box weight increases. Example: from Atlanta to Chicago, a two-pound package might cost $4.24 while a twelve-pound box can be sent for $8.04.

3. If you must travel, purchase super-saver tickets several weeks ahead, or travel between Christmas and New Year's. You could save a lot of cash by arriving home at noon on December 25, and would it really make any difference? Or consider catching a ride with a friend. Suggest that Junior enlist a pool of paying friends to help with expenses driving home from college.

4. Sending the same photocopied newsletter to keep everybody informed is a painless way to cut costs.

 *Bonus Idea 1:* If you have leftover cards and do not want to send the same ones next year, invite friends in for coffee and swap them after the holidays.

 *Bonus Idea 2:* Make your own greetings by recycling last year's best cards. Reuse the picture by cutting each card at the seam to make a picture postcard. On the flip side, write your message and the address, add a stamp and the word "recycled." In these days of concern for ecology and tight budgets, folks do respect the effort.

 *Bonus Idea 3:* To give inexpensive homemade cards with a spectacular touch, send a box or big manila envelope of your stamped, addressed, and sealed cards to one of the following interesting addresses for an eye-catching postmark: Postmaster, 535 Wood St., Bethlehem, PA 18016-9998; Postmaster, North Pole, CO 80809 (no red envelopes); Postmaster, Christmas, FL 32709-9998. The postmaster at these post offices will

put the postmark on your envelopes, then send them on their way.

Postmaster
North Polo, CO 80809
(NO RED ENVELOPES)

 *Bonus Idea 4:* Let the kids cut up pictures from old cards and reassemble them to make their own creative greetings, notepaper, bookmarks, collages, and mobiles. Punch a hole and thread a narrow ribbon through to make gift tags. Homemade cards and tags packaged twelve to a set in plastic bags and tied with a ribbon will disappear like magic at a bazaar!

A Last Word

When you waver and begin to backslide from your commitment to keep within a sensible Christmas budget, ask the local library to get a copy of the Alternatives Celebrations catalog from Alternatives, P.O. Box 429, 5263 Bouldercrest Road, Ellenwood, GA 30049. This catalog is full of ideas on how other families have made Christmas simpler, less expensive, and more meaningful. If they can do it, you can, too!

Bonus Idea: Take a look at spending money from God's point of view. Read the parable of the talents from Matthew 25:14-

30. This Scripture passage summarizes much of what the Bible has to say about money management. Ron Blue's book *Master Your Money* (Word, Inc.), may also help. In it, Blue draws several important precepts from the parable that we can recall each time we wonder what to do with money . . . or what it is doing to us.

Where Do I Get Money for the Christmas Crunch?

Even though you cut back on gifts for cousin Joe and Aunt Mamie, and have decided to share Christmas dinner expenses and forego all entertaining, and will be making most presents by hand this year, celebrating the holidays will cost money in one way or another. There will be scores of hidden incidentals—and almost nobody has the resources of Good King Wenceslas or the three kings of the Orient to pay for merry treats. Consumer financial experts say that, to be covered, you should have saved at least two-thirds of the amount needed to take care of holiday spending by the middle of November.

Some folks seem so organized that they can deposit money week after week in a savings account where it will be ready to be withdrawn just after Thanksgiving. Others are able to come up with the cash from a Christmas bonus. But many of us are like I was a few years ago. On April Fool's Day, I felt like the fool. I had a broken transmission in my car and no money to get it fixed because I was still paying for December bills!

Even if you are reading this in July, there is still time to save several hundred dollars. For extra funds, maybe you can:

1. Look into Christmas Clubs. An ordinary savings account sometimes does not offer a lot of incentive for stashing away weekly payday dollars. But the very name "Christ-

mas Club" helps you remember what you are doing. Pay yourself first by having money taken out of the paycheck each week, if you do not have lots of savings self-discipline. You will never see the money, let alone be tempted to spend it. Even better, you will come out with more than you had deposited because of accumulated interest. Savings of twenty dollars per week at 5 percent interest will yield approximately a thousand dollars a year; ten dollars a week nets about five hundred dollars.

2. Use the "fool yourself" tactic. If you get a raise sometime in the year, continue to manage on the old budget until Christmas, and ask that the extra funds be taken from each paycheck and banked in the credit union. Or whenever you pay off a big bill, like a car or credit card, continue to make payments, but to your savings account.

3. Tuck any change you receive (from the grocery store, dry cleaners, or elsewhere) into a separate change purse. At week's end, empty it into your savings account.

4. Utilize the "tack-on" tactic. Beginning in January, every time you buy stamps, purchase an extra book to lay aside in a big manila envelope marked "Christmas." By the time December arrives, there will be more than enough to mail all the Christmas packages and cards. The same idea can work for gifts. Whenever you purchase a dress and matching socks or a toy for one of your own children, purchase an extra to put away for nieces and nephews at Christmas.

5. Seal a quart canning jar, and cut a wide slit in the top. Label it "Christmas Can" and use it as a doorstop. Every time some-

body forgets to turn off a light when leaving a room, they must contribute a quarter (this saves on utility bills, too!). Or use a temperature bank, putting a little money in it according to the following: every day the temperature goes above 25 degrees—25 cents; 50 degrees—50 cents; 75 degrees—75 cents, and so on. The hotter the weather, the more money you save. Or set the jar atop the dresser in the bedroom so that husband and wife can deposit quarters for a whole year. The average couple will save fifty to seventy-five dollars. If you can keep the Christmas crunch clearly in mind, you may be able to stick in a ten- or twenty-dollar bill every other pay-day to avoid year-end money nightmares.

I found a glass bank fashioned like a cat in a dime store and called it my "Christmas Kitty." See-through banks allow the owner to check on savings progress at a glance. If I notice my kitty is not filling fast enough, I toss in a few more dimes and quarters next payday.

6. Compound Christmas savings by cutting corners else-where. Figure out how much you spend on what each week, then trim the fat from the grocery budget and other places to see how much can be freed up for holiday spending. If you buy lunch out (usually two to four dollars per day), decide to brown-bag for the month of November and put your savings into your Christmas fund. Or consider watching television a few nights instead of spending the nine to thirty dollars that it might cost for movie, concert, or sporting event tickets.

7. Be imaginative about how to earn extra money. One good cook made several hundred dollars catering holiday parties.

Another advertised her talents as a seamstress using the local paper and made a big dent in her holiday bills by doing alterations. There are usually many part-time jobs open during the holidays in department stores as gift wrappers and clerks. Perhaps you can offer childcare for shoppers or freelance some of your regular work. Consider working part-time in August when your schedule will not be as busy.

8. Sell something. Perhaps you own a few antique dishes or vases that now have considerable value. Is there a coin collection or an antique doll that you no longer want? Do you have a valuable hand-pieced quilt or some old, old musical instruments that nobody plays? Look in the classified ads under "wanted to buy" or advertise them yourself.

9. Get together with a neighbor or friend for a lively garage sale. The more items you have to tag, the more buyers are likely to attend. You will not only make a surprising sum, but you will also get rid of castoffs that clutter closets and shelves. The cost of advertising can be shared, too.

How to Take the Hassle Out of Shopping

Statistics show that merchants can count on American shoppers just like you and me to spend more than $25 billion during the jingle-bell season each year—and that's over and above regular buying! Most store owners reap about half of their annual income from holiday sales. Even if you decide to draw names for gifts, you will have to do other shopping for cards and wrappings, children's stocking items, fruit cake and cookie baking supplies, holiday dinner food, new clothes, hostess gifts, and things to freshen up the home.

Buying can be a hassle. When we enter stores from late October through December, we need all the "shopping smarts" we can get. We are bombarded with ads and items reflecting the behind-the-scenes Yule rule that commands, "Sell it or else!" Business places are sometimes packed elbow-to-elbow with discourteous and greedy shoppers, pickpockets, bawling babies in strollers, and inexperienced clerks. Counters and racks are overloaded with a confusing and tempting array of gorgeous or glitzy things that nobody would buy at other times—and prices are often outrageous. A magazine cartoon showed a sign inviting folks to "Come in and mangle with the crowds." For some, last-minute shopping and its accompanying panic prevails.

Believe it or not, there are simple ways to protect your equilibrium in the face of holiday shopping. You can begin by developing the attitude that Christmas is a wonderfully joyous downhill toboggan ride blessed with unfathomable spiritual riches, artistic elegance, chaos, and disorderly clutter. If you expect the topsy-turvy irregularity and hurry of the holidays—along with the exquisite satisfaction and fun—then you will not go around blaming everybody else for private feelings of discontent. You know the old saying, "If you can't beat 'em, join 'em!"

1. Anticipate all the joys of shopping that you can think of. For example, think about the brilliantly dazzling displays in big stores and on downtown lampposts; or the exciting hustle and bustle of folks getting ready; and the glorious heavenly background sounds of silver bells, chimes, and beloved carols. Like a wide-eyed tourist in a bazaar, you can enjoy the wondrous offerings of elegant merchandise piled high on handsome counters or displayed behind glass that are never seen at

other times. Anticipate the freebies along the way. There will likely be fascinating cooking demonstrations with delicious food samples, displays of what is new in cosmetics and household gadgets, high-tech items that you did not know existed, and even fashion shows or promotional contests that offer expensive prizes for dropping your name and address in a box. There is no reason not to get in the spirit of things! Remember, many folks don't have as much money, health, or energy to shop as you do—and many don't have a family to shop for, either. Aren't you fortunate?

2. Keep in mind that finding the "perfect gift" is a worthy goal, but it can also become a magnificent obsession that sends shoppers running off to nineteen different malls or confusedly ordering catalog merchandise that turns out wrong anyway. Let common sense be a guide as to how much time and effort you spend locating just the right thing. You may be pleasantly surprised when that gift you thought was just OK ends up bringing much joy to someone else's world.

3. Leave the kids at home when doing last-minute shopping. Nobody needs the hassle of whiny, uneasy youngsters, and you probably will end up buying unneeded items that they insist on. If kids must tag along, give them something to look forward to, such as a mystery stop (a few minutes at McDonald's playground or an ice cream store, or a choice of one toy from a favorite toy store).

   ■ Alternate Idea: Enlist cooperative older children to help out. While you do some shopping on your own, send them off with a specific list and price limits to purchase several

items. Insist that they select and wrap their own gifts for friends, teachers, scoutmasters, and sport coaches.

4. Shop when you are not exhausted. Wear comfortable clothes and low-heeled shoes. Give yourself a break every hour or so with lunch or coffee before weariness sets in. Tired shoppers are a lot more likely to buy whatever is available, regardless of cost or appropriateness, just to get the chore over and go home. Why not shop in spurts when you feel like it throughout the year?

5. Shop when nobody else does. Grab an umbrella and ignore the thunder shower or take a bus downtown on a snowy day. You quite probably will have a whole department store almost to yourself. You can make shopping a source of satisfaction rather than a burden by shopping early in the season, early in the day, or (for working people) before crowds arrive early in the evening. Phone to find out when stores and malls open (some businesses open as early as seven or eight o'clock during the holidays). If you plan to be one of the day's first customers, you probably will find plenty of easy parking and clerks who are far less frazzled. You will probably have more energy, too. Above all, avoid weekend shopping. Maybe the boss would let you take a day off work in October to get Christmas buying underway.

   ■ Alternate Idea: Pick up a gift every time you get a paycheck. Also, remember to keep eyes open for great gifts in shops you visit during vacation trips.

6. Avoid temporary stores or department store displays set up only for the season. They will probably be out of business on

December 26 if you need to return anything or take advantage of warranties.

7. Shop with a list. Knowing ahead of time what you want to buy saves lots of time and confusion. Be alert all year for gift ideas (and sales to match!) and jot down in a small notebook or on a sheet tacked inside a cupboard door the things others say they would like. Title the list "All Set for the Holidays!" Get the whole family involved. Even small children can come up with terrific suggestions, and your list will add to the wonderment and anticipation of Christmas.

   If you are making gifts, baking, or assembling a basket of things (such as various soaps, cosmetics, or kitchen gadgets) be sure to write each of these items separately on your list before leaving for the mall to save running back later. You may want to purchase several all-purpose gifts for those unexpected occasions when you need an extra gift.

8. To save energy, gasoline, and parking fees, take advantage of buses and subways. Take along sturdy shopping bags with handles. Utilize free delivery services offered by stores, but be aware that each store generally has its own rules and will charge a fee to deliver purchases under ten dollars. Use elevators instead of stairs. Shop top to bottom in stores if you will be visiting several floors. Working your way down from the top allows you to avoid fighting ordinary traffic that usually flows the other way. It also saves you from carrying first-floor packages upstairs. Call around to take full advantage of free department store shopping services (such as Macy's "By Appointment," which will do it all for you if you provide them with a list of items and the amount you want to spend

for each thing). If you live in a small town, try to locate an owner of a specialty shop who would lay out items you might be interested in so that they will be ready for you to view when you arrive.

9. Don't waste time running from mall to mall to check prices. Instead, use the yellow pages and the telephone for comparative shopping. Have model and style number, as well as color in mind for accurate comparison and to check availability of the exact items you want.

10. Plan a store-to-store shopping route ahead of time to get everything done in the shortest possible time and to avoid having to double back. Know the location of and the most direct route to specialty stores. It helps to know which floor you want, too, so phone ahead or ask at the information desk about the location of each store's various departments. Inquire about specific items, also. Coffee mugs might be in either the china or gift departments; bathroom sink accessories might be located in both linens and hardware.

11. Double-check all sales and charge account slips. Busy or temporary clerks are inclined to make more mistakes. Paying with cash is fastest; paying by check can be time-consuming and difficult.

12. Check merchandise by opening boxes before leaving the store, especially with sale items. Ask about additional charges for delivery, service, and installation when making a major purchase. As a timesaver, look for boxed or wrapped gifts displayed in hardware, housewares, cosmetics, and china departments.

Plan imaginative purchases from less crowded stores (such as sporting goods or stationery shops) to avoid bustling departments. Avoid crowds by shopping in unusual places. One woman who got tired of running from store to store retreated to the local museum and was pleasantly surprised to find a wealth of ideas in the gift shop: beautiful calendars, prints, jewelry, and books from all over the world. Now she goes there first because the choices are distinctive at any price, and it is never congested. I plan to order the Metropolitan Museum catalog to do at least part of next year's buying at home.

Harassed by holiday crowds, I took time off from downtown shopping one December to drop in at the huge Atlanta public library. Perusing the magazine racks, I saw plenty of periodicals I never knew existed on subjects ranging from auto racing and wood carving to square dancing and stamp collecting. There was literally a magazine to fit anyone and everyone on my shopping list, so I did the remainder of my Christmas shopping standing right there in the library! Best of all, nearly every magazine I wanted contained a convenient order form. My only task was to go home and write checks at my desk because most Christmas issues also offered to send a gala card informing the recipient that a subscription would be forthcoming in my name.

13. Make sure you understand the store's refund and return policy. No law requires businesses to make exchanges, although most do. Find out if a store gives cash refunds or if sale merchandise is returnable. Keep in mind that some things like swimsuits, stud earrings, bedding, and lingerie

may not be returnable for health reasons. Keep sales slips, hang tags, receipts, and all documents and warranties that come with purchases. This will save return hassles and help substantiate any later complaints. Save boxes, too. Some stores have identification codes taped inside the box so that customers cannot try to take back items bought elsewhere.

When making returns, call the customer service department to determine its location. Make returns as soon as possible after the holidays. Some merchants have limitations of two weeks or less. After that, many begin marking merchandise down and, if customers don't have sales slips and tags, will refund only the reduced price. Avoid asking for refunds during rush hours or at closing time. Many stores will accept returns without a sales slip, but will send the refund later in the mail. When a refund will be delayed, ask for a return receipt so you have something to show in case the check never arrives. (If you shop at a national chain store or order out-of-towner's gifts through a major catalog, unwanted items can probably be exchanged in the recipient's hometown.)

Catalog Know-How

Catalogs are a forty-eight-hour Santa Claus. Just about anything can be sent directly to your home (my husband orders specialty lumber for his home workshop to be delivered by UPS). Taking advantage of mail-order shopping can shave many stressful hours off of the time you spend in stores. Compare prices and don't forget to figure in shipping costs. Read descriptions of items carefully and make sure you know the approximate time it takes to

deliver the order. When ordering from catalogs, here are some things you should keep in mind:

1. Order early in the season to ensure there is plenty of time for delivery by Christmas, especially if the supplier is one you do not know or if the offer comes from television or magazine ads (allow six to eight weeks for these).

2. Never, *never* send cash or stamps. Pay by check or money order.

3. Keep a record of all orders, including the company's name and address, date of order, items requested, name of the publication where the order blank and display ad appeared, and canceled checks. This is the only way you will know where to send a complaint if the articles never arrive or if the order is incomplete.

4. Many catalogers deliver by UPS, so be sure to give your full street address and zip code. Using post office box numbers usually makes parcels undeliverable.

5. Some mail order companies reserve the right to substitute a comparable product if the first choice is not available. If you do not want a substitute, indicate such on the order form.

6. If you are running late, phone in the order and ask that articles be shipped by express mail directly to the recipient. If you think the gift still may not arrive in time, cut out an illustration and description of the item from the catalog, paste it inside a greeting card and write a note: "Better late than never. Your gift looks like this. It will be arriving soon."

Coping with Kids' Excitement, Crankiness, and Disappointment

"What child is this?" I once asked. Just when I needed my usually even-tempered five-year-old, Vicki, to be at her best, she whined about doing chores, complained about food, and was generally ornery. And she had been decking the halls and walls and everything else with crayons! On our way to the Christmas program at church, just as a glorious choir on the car radio was singing "Let nothing you dismay," she had a tantrum about buttoning her coat! I knew she was excited about Christmas and seemed worn out, yet she did not sleep as usual. Sometimes I wished she would quietly sit in a corner from Thanksgiving to Christmas, then join the family again after the gifts were opened. What can parents do to keep kids on an even keel when the atmosphere is so charged with excitement?

Young children do not quite understand the unusual holiday turmoil, but they are genuinely affected by the hustle and bustle and new sights and sounds. Kids may well be more vulnerable to seasonal tensions than adults are. They, too, have an unusually heavy round of Yule activities. There is so much tension in the anticipation and waiting, especially as they hear grown-ups planning wonderful meals, colorful parties, and visits from beloved relatives bearing exciting gifts. It takes Christmas so-o-o-o-o long to come!

Children sometimes feel uneasy and even lonesome as they sense the extra demands put on Mom and Dad. They become aware that their parents may not have as much time for them as usual. Quarrels and tears seem to come easier, adding a bittersweet note to the celebrating. Then there's the terrible letdown after presents are opened, which can create enough stress to make youngsters even more selfish and competitive about sharing with each other. But even in the face of all this, there is good

news for parents: although negative attitudes and actions and tantrums may be at a peak during the pre-Christmas rush, things will return to normal after the new year begins. Until then, use this checklist to help keep kids' hysteria to a minimum and make the holidays happier for everybody.

1. Try looking at things through your child's eyes. If you recognize that children are often overtired and overwhelmed by the anticipation of Christmas, it will help you be a little more tolerant of their excitability. Yuletide pressure is often acted out in many other homes, too, with more blow-ups, yelling, running, and pushing. Believe me, you are not alone. When flare-ups come, sit down and rock or read to the youngster until she gets back to normal. Talk over why the bad scene happened. Explain that next time things get troublesome and her behavior bothers others, she can go to her room and spend time calming down by herself. Keeping your voice low or gently removing an unruly child from a troubled situation and into another room can keep adults from adding to the general confusion.

   Allow for a little louder noise level than usual. It's Christmas! Save hard discipline for serious matters like when the youngster is jeopardizing the safety of herself or others. Still, you should not let down altogether. Remember, the assurance of at least some ordinary discipline will help keep the child's excitement from getting out of hand.

2. Prepare children ahead of time for holiday events. If you plan to visit relatives, have house guests, or attend special activities with the family, be sure to let youngsters know what to expect, what will happen, and why. Say it several times so the

real event will not come with so many surprises and to help small fry understand that following your directions is very important.

3. To relieve children's tension and make them feel a part of things, look for low-key ways to help. Busy hands really do make happy hearts. When a child is occupied, it does not seem to take so long for Christmas to come. Children who have been involved are less likely to be disappointed once Christmas is over, too. Yes, you could do things more quickly and easily yourself—but that is not what the season is all about! Kids who feel left out are unhappy and often become cantankerous. So tolerate their messes and mistakes. Spread out the season and assign easy duties. Let youngsters light Advent candles, set holiday tables, sew Christmas stockings, bring in fireplace logs, and help bake pies and decorate cookies

To channel excess energy in positive directions, allow children to do extra chores for pay to make money for gift buying. Tell them you need their help to dust the living room before an open house, or to seal envelopes, lick stamps, or place electric candles in all the windows. Older children can hang outdoor lights and address invitations. Remember, don't get preoccupied with making everything so perfectly beautiful that your kids feel they are in the way. Instead, enjoy their enthusiasm!

Bonus Idea 1: Try to relieve kids' stress by planning one simple celebration to please them for each of "The Twelve Days of Christmas." Festive days can include:

Polish the Silverware Day
Bake Fruitcakes Day
Ride in the Front (car) Seat Day
Stay Up as Late as You Want Day
Hear as Many Stories as You Want Day
Mom's Day
Don't Have to Get Dressed All Day Long Day
Christmas Carol Listening Day (Mom plays Christmas music
   on the stereo from breakfast to bedtime)
No Chores Day
Kids Get to Choose the Menu Day
Decorate Your Clothes Day (kids cut out holly designs from
   felt and help sew them on dresses, shirts, slacks and socks
   to make them real holiday standouts).

4. Keep your family routine as regular as you can. Kids thrive
on stable day-to-day schedules, especially when it comes to
mealtimes, afternoon naps, household chores, and activities such as being read to, nightly prayers, and homework
habits. Use bedtime to soothe and quiet after a big day. Try
to serve nutritious sit-down meals. Keep table time pleasant
and orderly and limit kids' intake of sweets to a minimum.
If they are given too many goodies, freeze some, marking
each packet with the child's name and promising a date
when packets can begin to be opened after the holidays.

5. Plan quiet times with children for listening to Christmas
music or rocking together at twilight and chatting awhile.
Tell a story about a Christmas when you were little. Was
there a time when you longed for a toy and did not get it?

Tell how you felt. Ask the child's feelings about the way your family celebrates Christmas. You may be surprised at what pleases your son or daughter most. Talk together about the good feelings that come from having everybody together. When the children are dressed in their nighties, perhaps you can turn off the rest of the lights and enjoy the tree together to calm down before bedtime.

6. Have plenty of solitary activities ready. If all of the children's Christmas books were packed away last year, there will be a supply of good reading that seems brand new. Kids can be put to work making terrific gift tags and placecards from last year's greeting cards, or cutting pretty snowflake decorations from construction paper or inexpensive paper lace doilies. Have children staple plain pages together, then write their own Christmas story to read to guests on December 25. Better yet, "commission" custom-made holiday drawings for special places in the house, over the fireplace, on a dining room wall, or in the front entrance hall. You can frame a blank paper with colorful cardboard and tell the youngster to draw inside the frame. Watch kids glow with pride when guests are told who made the fine wall hangings!

7. The less hype the better. Keep holiday priorities in order and the number of things going on at one time to a minimum. If Tuesday is the day when cousins are coming in at the airport, then delay the children's visit to Santa Claus. If you have spent all afternoon excitedly decorating the tree with the kids, wait until tomorrow to count piggy bank pennies or take youngsters shopping for Daddy's gift. After much soul-searching, one single mother bravely told her family that she

would not be attending the traditional December 24 dinner this year because things had gotten too hectic with her two-year-old starting tantrums and a pending job change. Her parents were disappointed, but this mom and her children needed the peace of staying at home.

8. Take care not to allow young children to attend too many evening events. Disrupted sleep habits, crowds of strangers, and too much hubbub invite irritability and high-strung antics. When the family will be out late, insist on a resting hour right after an early supper, even for school age youngsters. We often told our young daughters, "You don't have to go to sleep, but you must lie down for an hour until the clock strikes seven and it is time to get ready." Hiring a sitter or leaving babies and young children with amicable adults when you visit friends or have party guests in your home may be well worth the cost.

9. Emphasize the quieter religious events of Christmas. You need to help your children be as excited about the real meaning of Christmas as they are about the gifts they will receive. Now is the time to open the big family Bible and read together. Cozy up and tell your child what holiday symbols mean to you. Read litanies and pray together, even if you have not done it before. Provide books about why Jesus came. Kids are never really satisfied if the Yule focus is on toys alone. Though adults may not realize it, children often feel cheated without the added spiritual dimension in their celebrations.

10. Children enjoy being appreciated and will often be willing to go out of their way to do something thoughtful if encouraged

by adults. When kids talk only about what they want for themselves, shift the emphasis to Jesus and why he came. Talk together about the hidden meanings of Christmas, such as sharing, love, peace, and joy. This will help kids learn to ask, "What can I give?" instead of "What will I receive?"

If young children are wallowing in greed, send for a coloring book titled "The Joy of Christmas Giving" from Channing L. Bete Co., South Deerfield, MA 01373. Take the time to show your children ways to reflect Christ's love to others. One mom takes cookies and her ten-month-old baby and her eight-year-old son to a nursing home on Christmas Eve. The old folks always smile when they hold the baby and love to chat about school and joke with the older boy. Doing for others makes them all happy. Another mother allows her young children to print their names on the letter accompanying the Christmas money donation she makes to an organization that helps the homeless. She notes that it turns their attention to the deep satisfaction of giving.

11. When kids want too much for Christmas, tell those who are old enough to understand that you have a holiday budget and you need to stay within limits. Give realistic ideas about gifts by letting them know the approximate amount to be spent. This will help prevent ballooned expectations, which can result in Christmas morning resentment. Ask children to go over their request lists with you to reduce the most-wanted items to a favorite three or four. Promise at least one item, if you can. If they get more, all the better! The element of surprise makes up for sheer numbers of gifts. Most boys and girls are fair and will try to understand if you let them

know beforehand that expensive computers or talking teddy bears are out of the question. Set an early deadline for children's gift requests to avoid pressure from television ads that push very expensive items. Once the list has been agreed on, nothing more can be added.

When pushy ads do come on television, you may want to talk with youngsters about the kind of hard-sell advertising techniques commercials use and how much money toy manufacturers make. Help your children recall times when advertised toys were less than satisfying. Have them count the number of television ads for toys from three to six o'clock in the afternoon. Children probably will be astounded when they find they have been bombarded by as many as seventy-five commercials for games and playthings during the pre-holiday season. Show them that in nearly every case, the ad is effective enough to change attitudes to "I want that one!" Tell them that even adults are often brainwashed into thinking they "need" certain items.

You may want to break out of the toy syndrome by suggesting that this year, the family will be giving mostly non-store-bought gifts. Suggest that you will be giving things such as later bedtime privileges to teenagers. Children could give crocheted potholders or coupons good for a complete house vacuuming to a busy mother. Does the thought of doing this leave you feeling guilty? Try to recall your own intense anticipation and joy about giving your mom or dad a gift like a felt ink blotter, clay ash tray, or greeting card you made in second grade. Remember their heartfelt appreciation of your hard work? Once the idea of alternative gifts catches on, almost everyone enjoys the challenge.

12. It may be that, despite all your good planning, there are wistful, betrayed looks on the faces of your favorite little ones after all the presents are opened. Children may become sulky because dreams and fantasies about certain elaborate toys did not come true. Try not to take your children's complaints personally. Remember that a certain amount of letdown and disappointment—and perhaps even resentment—about what siblings or friends received is normal. It may be that the baseball mitt Jeffy requested in July just does not seem as exciting now that there is snow on the ground. That's just the way kids (and adults) sometimes are. One teacher says, "If the child is unhappy enough to get pouty and reject the gift completely, say something like, 'I'm sorry that you don't like my gift, especially since I really tried hard to please you.'" She advises parents to add quietly, "I will put it away on my closet shelf for now. You can let me know when you want it." Such an approach lets the youngster know that gifts are never deserved, but bestowed only because the other wishes to give away love. That lesson is much more important than trying to totally satisfy the boy or girl this one time.

If sulky and independent teenagers refuse to participate in the usual round of holiday activities, accept it without comment. Allowing them to make such decisions on their own without a scene increases the likelihood of their returning to the family fold later, when this cantankerous stage of development has passed. Teens generally go through a time of rebelling against family rituals—and almost everything else, it seems. But once the stage is over and they are on their own,

most fall right back into celebrating Christmas just the way Mom and Dad did "in the old days."

Beating the Holiday Blues

There are many holiday moods. In Atlanta, a sign outside a large church featured a seminar with the gloomy title of "How to Beat the Holiday Blues." Just down the street in a department store window, shimmering silver trees with cheerful lights twinkled to delight bustling, smiling shoppers and their happy children. Yes, the Yule season magnifies happiness. Unfortunately, it also magnifies blah and depressed feelings. Whether these emotions stem from loneliness, divorce, not enough money, family problems, sheer exhaustion, or whatever, they can seem larger than life in the light of the holidays.

As the mother of four, I loved the anticipation of Christmas, the kids' excitement, and the loving spirit the season generated. But along with the immense joy, I seemed to experience a downward pull of emotions as well. I sometimes had to pretend that I was enjoying myself. Often in December, moms especially note an unwanted undercurrent of being worn-out, of having too much to do, and of being overwhelmed by feeling that they alone are responsible for the family's Christmas happiness. We all expect so much of the holidays and are determined not to be disappointed.

One woman says, "Those traditional and expensive holiday table spreads that my parents and brothers and sisters expect are getting out of hand. Maybe I demand too much of Christmas, or maybe I let Christmas and family demand too much of me. How can I overcome the December blues?"

An Atlanta counselor offers help to those caught in this emotional bind. Here are this counselor's sensible suggestions for get-

ting rid of those "Bah, humbug!" feelings when you're hit with holiday overload during the Christmas–New Year's blitz. You may find that these ideas can help you restore some of the joy to your holiday season.

Plan-Ahead Calendar

Get a jump on Christmas by developing the attitude that you will plan for the holidays all year round. Determine what you really want to do and give, buy a calendar, and get started in January. Plan for the upcoming year so that last-minute things will not swallow up your hours. Pencil in any projects you need to begin early in the year, such as making gifts (i.e., afghans, clothing, a children's playhouse) or taking advantage of annual sales to make gift purchases. There's no need for you to go through shopping-mall neurosis the week before Christmas! Make shopping a breeze by marking off one day right after the Fourth of July, one day in September, and another day the first week in December to take advantage of seasonal bargains. Of course, these dates could change if you cannot get off work or if the flu attacks or Aunt Emmie visits unexpectedly—but at least your goal is down on paper. And don't wait until December to wrap gifts. Wrap them as you purchase them throughout the year, then tag them with numbers so snoopy kids and adults cannot guess whose the packages are.

Plan to update your Christmas card list in June and address Christmas cards while watching television on a hot August day. Or keep your cards in mind for an activity when you're shut in with the summer sniffles. Some people like to spread out the season by sending their greetings in January, when folks are more

likely to appreciate them. Consider writing a New Year's letter when things settle down instead of a Christmas letter in the midst of the chaos.

Schedule normally last-minute things for September, October, or November. Have the family photo taken or send money to the Salvation Army right after Labor Day. Plan to order from gift catalogs during the Thanksgiving weekend, when everyone else is wrapped up in football. Keep turkey week free for family, and let the children help trim the tree to fill vacation hours. Freezing cookie dough, fruit cakes, pie shells, and homemade fudge and buying for parties or making bows and favors for the Sunday school can all be done ahead. Breads can rise to the occasion in October and still retain fresh-baked tastiness in December. Schedule time during the summer or fall to check your holiday clothing (will you be able to don your gay apparel, cleaned and in good repair for social events?); iron linen tablecloths and napkins; and gather pinecones and nuts for wreaths. Why not schedule that overseas phone call to your sister right after Thanksgiving instead of on Christmas Day? What about a February dinner party when the kids are back in school and everybody is in midwinter doldrums? Call it something like the "Joneses' Delayed Christmas Bash."

As the year end approaches, begin to pencil in such activities as a concert of the *Messiah,* a visit to Aunt Mary, guest bedroom preparations, the Christmas party at church, house cleaning, beauty appointments, and final dates to mail packages. (Hint: It is OK to mail gifts by December 1, or even on Memorial or Labor Day, and mark them "Do Not Open until Christmas." Wrap them so spectacularly that they will be an exciting mystery for a long time on the closet shelf.)

One dad admits, "In December, my wife and I sat down together to examine our holiday schedules and found only two open nights to spend at home." If your family yearns to spend more time together, then be sure to write in specific "family only" activities on your holiday planner. You may even want to pencil in a reminder to ask your boss at work if you might take part of your vacation during the holidays.

There now! As you use your calendar for year-round Christmas strategy, your mind will stop whirling and projects will begin to fall in place. You will finally be able to sing the "Hallelujah" chorus along with everybody else. No more Christ-MESS! You will begin to feel confident that you are definitely on top of things.

Tame Your Expectations

Do not expect to be everything to everybody. One mom says, "There is this phantom picture in my head of a *Better Homes and Gardens* 'house beautiful,' complete with exquisite handmade decorations, perfectly behaved children dressed in cranberry velvet quietly enjoying wooden rocking horses and handmade doll houses, huge silver plates of home-baked Christmas goodies in every room and an exquisitely browned turkey stuffed with exotic sweet potato dressing and served on finest china to a smiling family. I have felt more weary than merry trying to measure up. After years of complaining about the heavy demands on me, I have concluded that my family does not want a super-mom with endless energy to plan every detail and make kitchen floors look like mirrors. They just want a quiet wife and mother who will let the holidays unfold and guide them happily through without foisting unhappy routines on everybody. I have freed myself of the

stress of performing a blizzard of chores in an outstanding way. Instead I simply select a few places where I shine and put my efforts into them."

I once asked several of our children and grandchildren what they remembered and liked best about our celebration. The oldest daughter smiled, "The gumdrop trees we made together." Others said, "Driving around to look at house decorations," and, "The whipped cream salad served at Christmas dinner." The simple things really are the most enjoyable. The activities that once took a major part of my time and energy, like making elaborate table centerpieces or putting together the new wild rice dressing recipe with fifteen ingredients went almost unnoticed. Maybe you cannot do it all this Christmas either. If so don't despair. Instead, here are a few tips on surviving the season by doing less:

1. Trim kitchen chores by baking only half of the holiday favorites. If you need more goodies, buy six dozen cookies and a pound cake from the deli. Order a precooked turkey or eat Christmas dinner out.

2. Invite holiday guests for breakfast or brunch instead of dinner and serve a special dessert for which you are famous. Or consider not entertaining at all this year. Remind yourself that it is OK to let down a little.

3. If you must cook, substitute easier, quicker recipes. If this is an unusually busy Christmas, make all your baked Christmas goodies from prepackaged mixes. There are plenty to choose from, and they all taste great.

4. Find grocery stores that still deliver without charge to save on shopping (and standing in checkout line) time.

5. Ask a neighbor to cut a Christmas tree and bring it back for you when he does his own. Next year, it is your turn. Or phone a nursery and have them deliver a live potted tree.

6. Never mind the tree's teddy bear theme and the fancy lace fans and pearl strings hung other years as exotic decorations. Small children are very understanding and will be just as delighted with a few sparkling strings of lights. Decorate only the tree and front door and forget candles and greenery in every window, or stringing nine hundred lights across the front porch like the neighbors do.

7. Are you frantically trying to finish a last-minute gift? Instead of making yourself crazy with an unrealistic deadline, put away your materials and send a note along with a clipping or drawing of what the gift will look like when it is completed. In the note, promise you will deliver this delightful present on March 30 (or some other convenient date).

8. Buy theme gifts for everyone, such as books or exercise gear. This will enable you to do all your shopping in one or two stores. One Atlanta woman always sends her two sisters identical gifts, which eliminates all that time spent searching for the perfect present for each person.

9. Combine several things into one. For example, make your annual party a tree-trimming event. Guests will be delighted to be invited and the tree gets decorated by many willing hands.

10. Just say no and cancel the headache-makers. Your well-being is more important than the office Christmas party. If you're

feeling overwhelmed, give a firm negative answer when asked to be chairman of the country club decorating committee (even if you have done it for years and your artistic talent surpasses everyone else's!). Postpone buying a puppy or gerbil or any other living creature that requires training or care until later or even until a birthday.

11. Gain control over extra obligations by letting up on a few regular activities such as bowling, bridge games, or club meetings. Maybe you could find a substitute to teach your Sunday school class during December. And skip sending "obligation" gifts to people who probably don't even expect to receive anything.

12. Ask good friends to join their party with yours for half the work and maybe more fun.

Call In the Reserves

Utilize all the help you can get. Your most important job is to keep on being loving and giving, but that doesn't mean you have to become everybody's servant. Ask firmly for help without showing angry outbursts. Assign tasks to the kids and post a "to do" list on bedroom doors early in the day or week. Older children are often willing to take younger ones to dental appointments or make trips to the store. Others can clean guest rooms or call relatives about clothing sizes or phone in orders to catalog stores. Maybe you can give each child a title like "Errand Runner" or "Phone Mate" or "Postman" (to stamp envelopes or stand in line at the post office). This will make jobs easier to assign when they come up. One year, I enlisted

my fourth grader to wrap gifts, and taped a note on each that read "Custom-wrapped by Mary Jo."

Take Time for You

Make a little peace on earth for yourself. Give yourself permission for time alone, without guilt, to do what *you* want to do. Early in the 1900s, John Foster wrote, "If I had the power of touching a large part of mankind with a spell, amid all this inane activity, it should be this short sentence, 'Be Quiet, Be Quiet.'"

Maybe you could have one of the neighborhood children babysit while you are in the house so you can flop on the bed and listen to soft music, give yourself a facial, or put your feet up and sip a cup of peppermint tea. On a workday, enjoy midwinter sunshine by taking a fitness walk during a noon hour break. Other ideas include meditating on quieting passages from Psalms, slipping the headphones on to soak in your favorite music, or do anything else that will help refresh and energize you. Remember, you have to take care of yourself. No one else can, or will, do the job as well.

Stamp Out Stress

Be creative about managing stress. Every time feelings of "Poor me" arrive, stamp them out mentally with an imaginary "cancel" stamp. He who laughs, lasts. Cultivate a sense of humor about your arthritis twangs or impending surgery. Laughter lifts the spirit and even changes things. If you remember nothing else this season, remember this: *Laugh!*

Laugh when the Christmas cookies turn too crispy because they are left too long in the oven. Laugh when the tree falls over,

when you cannot locate the decorations, or when the kids develop chicken pox on Christmas Eve. Laugh when you feel the pressure coming on. You may be amazed at the way it helps.

In addition to laughter, do something to divert your attention from the stress. Put up a bird feeder and watch what happens. Renew an old friendship. Go out and look at the stars. Play frisbee with the dog. Daydream over travel brochures. Put off dealing with routine problems. They can wait. Clear your worry calendar and refuse to tackle major issues, even if they are in-laws, job problems, hurt feelings, or whatever. You can deal with those things later, when you're less fatigued. For now, it's Christmas!

Savor the Season

Find something to anticipate. Take hold of joy! Stop, look, and listen for Christmas. Consider all the wonderful possibilities of the season and jot them down. Remind yourself that many of the best blessings are ahead, even for you. Recall good times past and thank God for each one. Notice the good things other people are doing. Savor the season—the laughter of a small child, the joy of a family time together, the magic of magnificent church choirs, the wonder of the Christmas story, the never-ending miracle of God's love.

Watch Your Health

Keep reasonable health strategies. Take care of yourself by getting extra sleep, sticking to exercise routines, and eating balanced meals. Skip handy snacks, candy, or chips and dips. Don't allow yourself to be coerced or coaxed into taking holiday goodies you do not want. Smile when hosts or hostesses hold out

plates of goodies, tell them that everything looks wonderful and
you appreciate their giving spirit . . . then gently refuse. Consum-
ing all those extra calories can only make you feel worse. Something else to keep in mind is that caffeine and alcohol are energy
sappers. If you overindulge, you will regret it—and a hangover
can put a damper on Christmas for everyone around you.

If you have a medical problem, keep following the doctor's
orders. If a new one develops, do not put off seeing a physician
until after the holidays. Good health is an integral part of enjoying
the holidays. Don't take chances with something that can be so
easily—and seriously—damaged.

Slow Down

Slow down a little, just because you feel like it. Drive in the slow
lane on the freeway. Shut off television and radio. Talk more slowly
and eat at a more leisurely pace. Remind yourself that nothing
really *has* to be done by a certain time. The world will not come
crashing down on you if you don't do it all. Truth is, friends and
family probably won't even notice if something isn't done! Even if
they do, they quite likely will understand. If someone should criti-
cize or complain, don't let it bother you. You know what you can
and cannot realistically do. It's more important for you to do your
best than for you to meet someone else's unrealistic expectations.
Remember, Christmas is a time to focus on God's unconditional
love for us—not on the ways we don't measure up.

Give Yourself a Break

Allow yourself to be human. It is difficult to forgive ourselves for
occasional weariness and discouragement, especially when we

reason that "everybody else" seems to have great enthusiasm. Don't kid yourself. All of us get tired and frustrated by too much to do and by dealing with the daily problems that remain, even at Christmas. Maybe *anybody* in your shoes would be in a down mood, even your most cheerful acquaintance. Give yourself full credit for all the planning and caring you have been able to give. Ask for a hug. Claim Philippians 4:13: "I can do everything God asks me to with the help of Christ who gives me the strength and power." But keep in mind that it is *Christ* who does the strengthening, not you. If you rely on his endless supply rather than on your dwindling one, you will find yourself enjoying the season a great deal more.

Be Kind

Christmas is a gentle season, so do not let strained family relationships spoil it. Consider just accepting an uncle who drinks a little too much or an overly talkative aunt or a cousin who seems selfish and bossy. The holidays are stressful enough without trying to do something you cannot: change other people. God is the one who will change others, not you. You cannot change anyone but yourself. Realize that Christmas, with all its built-in stresses, may not be the right time to encourage your husband to pay more attention to a difficult mother-in-law or to harass Mom about following her diabetic diet more strictly. If you must make a weekend visit with a brother whose wife always runs the show and makes you feel uneasy, why not try concentrating on whatever positive traits you find? There are no perfect families. So yours probably is as normal as most. People too often forget what they mean to each other—in spite of the imperfections.

In fact, why not take advantage of the differences? If your sister married a Chinese Buddhist, let the different cultural backgrounds enrich the holiday. Make finding out about the other person a topic of interesting conversation. Ask about different beliefs or traditions. Do what you can to help your children to feel at home with folks from other traditions, nationalities, and denominations. Kids can learn to respect others without taking on their life-styles or ideals.

Remember Your Faith

Use the holidays to grow in your faith. Call the church down the street to ask for reading material. Pick up a book of daily devotionals. Spending time with the author of peace will stabilize your thoughts and emotions and bring an element of calm into your life that will rub off on those around you. Perhaps the daily time with God that you begin during this Christmas season will become a permanent part of your life. It is, without a doubt, the best investment you can make.

Remember the Reason

Understand the purpose behind the preparations. If you're not clear as to what the real reason for the Christmas season is, read this letter that Diane M. Busch of West Virginia sent to *Today's Christian Woman* magazine:

A Gift of Love

When December arrived last year, my husband and I began making lists of what we needed to do to prepare for Christmas—all our shopping, wrapping gifts, mailing cards, baking,

and decorating. It seemed overwhelming. Our little daughter asked why we were doing all these things, and our answer to her question gave us a new purpose for the work: We were preparing a birthday party for Jesus, the most important person who ever lived.

We viewed our "chores" differently after that discussion. Buying gifts became a wonderful way to show others that we love them as Christ first loved us. Mailing Christmas cards was an excellent opportunity to share the real meaning of Christmas and witness about Jesus and his love. Decorating our home and baking helped us show hospitality and enjoy Christian fellowship.

On Christmas Eve before our service at church, we held a special Christmas dinner for our extended family. We had a birthday cake and sang "Happy Birthday" to Jesus, a tradition that served as a reminder of the real reason for Christmas.

This year we will again remember the purpose behind our preparations as we look forward to celebrating the most important birthday of all.

Don't Look Back

No looking back! Be glad for *today's* blessings. If you are mired in the Santa myth, or caught up in "if only" fantasies ("If only Jim were here, things would be great!"), or if you expect to relive Christmases past with figgy pudding and sleigh bells in the snow, you will only be disappointed. Fighting to live in the past is a losing battle. Accept the real challenge of making the most of the holidays in today's circumstances.

Gloria Gaither, a well-known speaker, lyricist for the Bill Gaither Trio, and author, accepted this challenge. In her book, *Let's Make a Memory,* which she wrote with Shirley Dobson (copyright © 1986; Word Books, Dallas), Gaither tells how, one special winter's day, she handled life's new season of being a grown-up child and celebrating with her aging mother and father:

> If everything special and warm and happy in my formative years could have been consolidated into one word, that word would have been *Christmas.* So, by the time the building blocks of my days had piled themselves into something as formidable as late adolescence, Christmas had a lot to live up to.
>
> Christmas, by then, meant fireplaces and the bustle of a big excited family, complete with aunts, uncles and cousins. It meant great homemade bread and cranberries bubbling on the stove, pumpkin pies and turkey. It meant Grandma's cheery voice racing to be the first to holler "Christmas Gift!" as we came in the door. It meant real cedar Christmas trees, handmade foil ornaments, and lots of secrets. It meant enfolding in the arms of our great family the lonely or forsaken of our village who had no place to go. It meant all the good and lovely things we said about Christmas being in the heart and the joy being in the giving.
>
> Then came that other year.
>
> There were many things that conspired, as it were, to bring me to the laboratory situation in which I would test all my so glibly accepted theories. Grandma was gone, leaving in my heart a vacuum that wouldn't go away. My sister was

married now and had the responsibility of sharing her holidays with her husband's people. The other relatives were far away. After a lifetime of serving in the ministry, Daddy had that year felt directed to resign his flock with no other pastures in mind and "wait on the Lord." Since I was away at college, just beginning my first year, I wasn't there when my parents moved from the parsonage to the tiny cottage at the lake which a concerned businessman had helped them build. Nor was I prepared that winter day for the deserted barrenness that can be found in resort areas built only for summertime fun.

There was no fireplace. There was no bustle of a big excited family. Gone was the sense of tradition and history that is the art of the aged to provide, and gone was the thrill of the immediate future that comes with the breathless anticipation of children.

The dinner was going to be small, for only the three of us, and there just wasn't any ring in the brave attempt at shouting "Christmas Gift!" that Mother made as I came in the door. Daddy suggested that because I'd always loved it, he and I should go to the woods to cut our own tree. I knew that now, of all times, I could not let my disappointment show. I put on my boots and my cheeriest face, and off through the knee-deep snow we trudged into the Michigan woods. My heart was heavy, and I knew that Mother was back at the stove fighting back the tears for all that was not there.

There was a loveliness as the forest lay blanketed in its heavy comforter of snow, but there was no comforter to

wrap around the chill in my heart. Daddy whistled as he chopped a small cedar tree. (He always whistled when there was something bothering him.) As the simple tuneless melody cut through the silent frozen air, I got a hint of the silent burdens adults carry, and for the first time felt myself on the brink of becoming one. So as I picked up my end of the scraggly, disappointingly small cedar, I also picked up my end of grown-up responsibility. I felt the times shift. I was no longer a child to be sheltered and cared for and entertained. My folks had put good stuff in me. Now as I trudged back through the snow, watching the back of my father's head, the weary curve of his shoulders, his breath making smoke signals in the morning air, I vowed to put some good stuff back into their lives.

The day was somehow different after that. We sat around our little table stringing cranberries and making foil cut-outs. But this time it was not the activity of a child, but sort of a ceremonial tribute to the child I somehow could never again afford to be, and to the people who had filled that childhood with such wealth and beauty.

Let the beauty and magic that today holds—and it *does* hold some, for every day holds the presence of a loving God—fill and refresh you. Accept the challenge; make it a point to "put some good stuff" into your todays. You won't regret it. And you may even discover the best Christmas you have ever had!

Spending Christmas Alone without Being Lonesome

Ho! Ho! Ho! 'Tis the season to be jolly.

"Not for me!" one distraught woman said. "I want to cancel Christmas. I am a thousand miles away from my family, just divorced, trying to have a merry little time by myself. I hate it. Christmas is second-rate without people around."

Maybe you, too, have recently lost a spouse through separation, divorce, or death. Perhaps you have just been transferred to a new job far away from friends and family. Maybe you are unmarried or living alone for other reasons. Millions of people will spend the Yule season by themselves, though most might confess that they would rather share Christmas pleasures with somebody they enjoy. Holiday blues often move in quickly with the reds and the greens if you believe that everybody should go back home for the holidays and that nobody should spend December 25 alone.

As difficult as it may be, it's time to stop glorifying past holidays and the traditional picture-perfect family image of a happy homemaker mother, a nine-to-five father, and cherubic children all gathered around a crackling Christmas Eve fire. In today's world, only 4 percent of the family population in America can claim to be this "traditional" kind of family! There are many other family systems today: singles, families with one parent, families faced with divorce or separation, combined families with stepparents or stepsiblings, couples without children, those with or without children whose spouses have died, and many more. With these undeniable facts facing us, isn't it time to accept that whatever kind of family system you have is OK?

Things have changed. Distance may deprive us of those we love, but it also can free us to develop new traditions and give us

freedom to customize Christmas Day and spend it any way we wish. Emerson once said, "To the wise, life is a festival." Christmas is what you make it, so focus on making this year's holiday the best ever as you read through the following ideas for spending the day by yourself.

1. Take a morning shower, then shave or put on makeup (as appropriate). Dress in nice clothes and create a Dickens-style dinner. You deserve this kind of meal, so don't short yourself. Serve food on your best china and use the prettiest tablecloth. No paper napkins! Do not forget a lovely centerpiece and candles to make your holiday table glow with warmth. Why not take a snapshot of your wonderful "before" spread to send back home to the folks or to show off at the office? Listen for the church bells at noon.

2. Be kind to yourself. Fill your home with splendor. Buy six poinsettias to bank against one wall and deck the halls inside and out as if you expected a dozen guests. Do you enjoy receiving gifts? Why not receive some of your own—from you? Wrap up Christmas presents for yourself, items you have wanted for a long time. You deserve nice things. A microwave oven? Some small appliance (i.e., an electric can opener or coffee pot) to ease kitchen work? What about a mini-television set for the bedroom or a special pair of fashion texture stockings with designs woven all over? How about new slippers and a robe, an all-wool argyle sweater and matching socks, or a bright red vest to match a gray flannel suit?

3. Hole up in your apartment all day with a stack of magazines, crossword puzzle books and a special picture puzzle. Warm

your heart and toes by curling up by the fire with a hot cup of tea and an armful of library books on a subject you have always wanted to know about. Reread favorite classics such as *Jane Eyre* and *Uncle Tom's Cabin.* Load the freezer with black walnut cake or French ice cream for extra holiday kindness to yourself.

4. Read over each Christmas card and letter again and pay special attention this time to the good tidings of comfort and joy. Sometimes we quickly rip open the volume of holiday mail without concentrating on the message. (You may even want to wait until Christmas Day to open your cards. As they arrive, you could place them, unopened, in a basket or box decorated with red and green ribbons and bows.) String opened cards over a doorway or on the tree for a festive decoration that will remind you of the folks who are thinking about you.

5. Focus on allowing yourself time to simply be. Daydream away a few hours in a frothy whirlpool or bubble bath. Take a sight-seeing ride in the country or bundle up and take a long walk. Could you locate Joy Street or Holiday Lane? Breathe in crisp air or enjoy the patter of rain on an umbrella. Admire winter evergreens in the yard and enjoy the fresh feeling of snow on your face. Feel the rhythm of your own moving feet and your brisk heartbeat. Be especially aware of whatever measure of good health you have. Breathe a prayer of thanks for freedom.

6. Write a letter to an old high school or college pal, or to a relative you have not seen in years. It will be Christmas all over again when you receive a reply. Repot plants or start an

indoor green dish garden. Every time you water it, you will be reminded how creative you were the time you spent Christmas alone.

7. Borrow and view videotapes that you have wanted to see for a long time. Watch television schedules for wonderful movie oldies like *Miracle on 34th Street, Holiday Inn,* or *It's a Wonderful Life*. Or you could treat yourself to a movie at a local theatre. Maybe you would enjoy a rerun of a childhood favorite like *Snow White.*

8. Putter around the house. Ask yourself, "What do I want to do today?" So often, we ask instead, "What *must* I get done today?" Perhaps you can knit, do woodworking, catch up on entries in a journal, write poetry or begin your memoirs. Play Christmas music all day as a backdrop to whatever you choose. Regard the hours as a gift of time to catch up on exercise, sleep, or do absolutely nothing. In this harried and hurried world, time for yourself is hard to come by. Enjoy!

9. Slay the demon of boredom by trying something new. Put together a kit. Cut out your first dress pattern or sew up a cheery hostess apron. Make bagels or graham crackers just because hardly anyone else does. Dye a faded blouse. Blow eggs and color them to hang on the tree. Look in the paper for special Christmas Day events you have never attended before.

10. Make New Year's resolutions or a calendar of plans for the upcoming year. Pencil in things like enrolling in new classes or tentative vacation ideas. If you are getting fat right along with the proverbial Christmas goose, plan a diet.

11. Helping someone else is a great cure for loneliness and self-pity. Is there some good deed you could do? Why not find someone who has a need and help out. Maybe you can copy a few of Nita Schuh's ideas. Here she shares about her "Merry Month of Christmas":

Thanksgiving had been difficult enough—how would I ever make it through Christmas? I couldn't go running to family or friends again, or take a getaway cruise. No. The time had come to pick up the threads of losing Joe. Though his death had left me feeling empty, like a fresh mountain stream gone dry, somehow I knew I would have to find a way of restoring the joy to this holy season—without my husband. It pained me to think that his bubbly spirit would not be around to make the holidays full and complete. I had to accept that things could never again be the way they used to be. I had to let go of "us." I had to begin reaching forward—on my own.

December was here and Christmas was right around the corner. Nothing came to my mind. My spirits were heavy when I walked into the kitchen one morning. It was three weeks till Christmas, and I hadn't done a thing. Between sips of hot coffee, my eye suddenly caught my wall calendar hanging on the refrigerator door. The month of December peered back at me, the boxes glaringly empty until December 25th, circled in red. I felt ashamed.

I got up and took the calendar down, placing it on the table in front of me. "No more wasting time," I told

myself. *"Right now* I will expectantly look forward to Christmas."

I picked up a pencil, and at the top of the calendar I wrote, "The Merry Month of Christmas," feeling anything but merry as I did so. Then, hoping for something inspirational to plan for, I began to idly fill in the blank squares: make cookies for Cousin Edie (89 years old, blind, and in a nursing home); baby-sit while Nancy (a friend's daughter) Christmas shops; address and mail Dad's cards; share holly and other greenery from my garden with Virginia, my apartment-dweller friend; have a tea for widowed friends in my neighborhood; and so on.

I felt lighter. There was nothing spectacular, but before I knew it, nearly every date had been filled in and the margins of the calendar were full and overflowing with scribbled notes and ideas as well.

As the days unfolded and I began to actually do the things I had jotted down, an excitement for each day filled me in an unbelievable way. Soon my problem became, "How shall I get all of these things done?" I didn't want to leave *anyone* out! I could hardly believe that only a few weeks ago I had been so lonely I didn't even want to think about Christmas. Now I wished I had more time before Christmas arrived!

In the end, I did have plenty of time to do the things I had planned, and to enjoy the company of my friends. And when the month was over, I discovered it had, indeed, been the "Merry Month of Christmas" after all!

That was four years ago. Each year since, I've repeated

my tradition in some form, and it has become more and more a time of happy anticipation as well. And I know Joe would have been proud of me. What is even more pleasing is that my little idea caught the imagination of others. Last year one friend called to tell me, "Remember when you celebrated all the month of December, Nita? Well, I'm doing that, too. . . ."

Maybe some of you might like to join us this year. If so, right now, take your December calendar and at the top of the page write, "The Merry Month of Christmas." Begin to fill in the squares with your own ideas . . . that's how it all began for me. The simple practice of making commitments brought rich rewards in learning to give—when I thought I had nothing—and in the end, made my Christmas full and complete.*

12. Dogs love Christmas, too. If you and a pet are sharing Christmas, tie a big red ribbon around the animal's neck to help celebrate. Share thoughts and feelings aloud with your pet. Why not knit an adorable Yule stocking and bake up some of these dog biscuit treats to drop in along with a new toy or leash?

Cheesy Dog Biscuits

2 cups all-purpose flour
1¾ cups shredded Cheddar cheese
2 tablespoons dried garlic
½ cup cooking oil
3 tablespoons water

*Reprinted with permission from *The Guideposts Family Christmas* book. Copyright © 1980 by Guideposts Associates, Inc., Carmel, NY 10512

In a large bowl, combine, flour, cheese, garlic. Cut in oil with a pastry cutter until mixture is the consistency of coarse corn meal. Add water until mixture forms a ball. Use a food processor, if you like.

Roll out mixture to about½-inch thickness and cut out in the shape of a bone or cut with ordinary cookie cutters. (Trace around a store-bought dog biscuit if you cannot find a cutter.)

Bake on ungreased cookie sheet in preheated 400 degree oven for 12-15 minutes, or until biscuits are slightly brown on the bottom. Cool on wire rack. Refrigerate.

13. Put a song in the air right where you are. Sing Christmas carols aloud and listen to the words. *Really* pay attention. It will enhance the significance of today's celebration.

14. Prepare him room. Take advantage of today's quieter pace for fellowship with God. Maybe you can begin at breakfast with a prayer of thanksgiving for the gift of life God has given you. Rather than focusing on what you did not receive or what you cannot do, list on paper past and present blessings. Someone wisely said that if we expect to gain nothing more than what God has already given us, anything will be a welcome surprise. Recall at intervals all day long that even though you have moments when you hunger for the warmth of a group or a sense of belonging, you are never alone. Remind yourself over and over whose birthday it is, and that God is with you.

Plan and look forward to short blocks of time every couple

of hours for communion with the Immanuel of Christmas. During those times, read Scripture and pray. Spend time praying for the world's grief, the homeless and hungry, soldiers stationed at lonely outposts, struggling missionaries, for those in bondage to drugs and crime, for troubled friends, for peace around the world, and for our president and other world leaders attempting to achieve this peace. Here is your chance to give the gift of supportive prayer to others and transform your day into a rich spiritual experience.

15. Spend time thinking about how to spend next year's holidays. What traditions would you like to begin? Did you like this year's solitude so well that you have decided to be by yourself again? Plan a heavenly holiday getaway to a place you have long wanted to visit. Rent a condo at the ocean's edge and walk the beach gathering shells in the afternoon, or nap in the sunshine and treat yourself to a fresh lobster or shrimp dinner. Maybe you will see three ships come sailing in! Or, consider going to a cabin near the ski slopes for a day of skiing and ice skating, and an evening warming yourself before the clubhouse fire with other holiday sports enthusiasts.

Bonus Idea: Take a child with you. Not only will you have good company, but a fresh and enthusiastic outlook about any side tours you take and plenty of excuse to indulge yourself in childish pleasures like making sand castles or eating triple-dip ice cream cones.

16. Maybe none of the magic of Christmas is reaching you, despite all your courageous efforts to enjoy the upcoming holiday alone. If you are not particularly looking forward to being by yourself, timidity will get you nowhere. Venture out in new ways to boldly connect with others. It takes a bit of courage to invite someone you hardly know for dinner (someone who might reply, "Sorry, but I'm flying to be with my ten brothers and sisters in California"). Even if you are turned down or if your guest does not have a good time at your house, it is not the end of the world. Head out in a new direction. Besides, both of you just might have the best Christmas ever.

Instead of going back home as usual, a single professional living alone in a big city could invite parents or a widowed mother or father for the holidays. Mom or Dad would probably love the idea of spending time with one of their children. And you may find that you enjoy the feeling of being a grown-up friend to parents instead of a kid going home for Christmas. There are bound to be a few laughs and lots of kidding around about kitchen skills (or the lack thereof), but your turkey may be the best ever. Maybe your guests will enjoy themselves so much they will decide to stay over a few days to finish seeing the city sights.

A lonely retired schoolteacher or unmarried woman or new divorcée could lift holiday spirits by inviting single-again friends over for a Christmas Eve chowder supper and to spend the night. Each can bring a present appropriate for anybody. In the morning, there will be plenty of people to cel-

ebrate and open gifts together and lots of fun jesting about who makes the best French toast for breakfast.

Other ideas to reach out for friends:

- Invite a friend who is suffering from discontent to camp out with you on Christmas Day.

- Volunteer to work the holiday shift for a coworker who wants to be with family.

- If you live in an apartment, slip notes under anybody's door whom you think is home, inviting all who can come for Christmas night hors d'oeuvres. If you have too much food, just freeze leftovers for another gathering.

- Look around at work or church for someone else who may be alone. Never mind age or other differences. Ask if the person would like to share expenses for a lavish dinner at your house. Or ask him or her over to see your gifts and have coffee on Christmas night. The other person may be craving fellowship as much as you are.

- Invite a separated or divorced mother and her children from church to join you for good food and Christmas night devotionals.

- If you can locate enough singles, invite them over for Christmas night snacks to talk about setting up a regular Monday night fellowship dinner group.

- If you have brothers, sisters, or close friends, maybe you can call and ask to spend Christmas Day with them for this year only. Offer to bring your sleeping bag. Want to

stay longer? Perhaps someone with kids needs a baby-sitter for a day or two while they get away. It will give you a chance to get to know the children, too.

■ Consider hosting a Christmas Coffee for friends and neighbors. Suggest on the invitation, and as you talk with neighbors, that everyone bring something they've been doing with their hands, such as crafts, or talk about another aspect of themselves. You may be quite surprised by the results. Fascinating crafts and hobbies may be shown, and other "gifts" may be discovered, as well. Perhaps one of you is an accomplished pianist and will play a piece for the rest. Others may sing special songs or discover similar interests and involvements.

Serve Christmas treats with the coffee, and weave the Christmas message in your conversations whenever appropriate. You undoubtedly will have had an excellent morning worth everyone's while, while reaping a harvest that will last for eternity.

■ Do you have an upstairs neighbor? Here is how one lonesome woman, Terri Castillo, made room for Christmas in the big city.

The subway car screeched to a halt and an unusually cheerful voice piped, "82nd Street, Jackson Heights—and Merry Christmas, everyone!" Wrapping my scarf around my neck, I stared at the happy faces glowing under the bright subway lights. Women and children clung excitedly to colorfully wrapped boxes tied with shiny ribbons. Men chatted merrily, exchanging holiday greetings. The

festive scene was unlike the usual somber subway rides. Tonight was Christmas Eve and the air was electric. For everyone, that is, but me.

This was my first Christmas in New York City. Leaving my family and friends back in Hawaii, I had moved here several months earlier—a young woman curious about the "Big City." It promised to be an exciting life, but it was sometimes a lonely one, and making friends wasn't easy. I'd hoped to spend the holidays with another young woman I had met in my apartment building, but she had been unexpectedly called home for Christmas. Now, having no other friends living nearby, I would spend Christmas alone.

As happy spirits escalated around me, I felt more and more homesick. "This is supposed to be a family celebration," I kept telling myself. "How can I celebrate Christmas without my family?" All I could think of was the empty room waiting for me, the television set my only company.

I slushed through the buildup of snow on the subway platform and trudged down the icy steps leading to the street below. Strings of twinkling lights crisscrossed overhead along the avenue forming arches of stars against the dark night. From the little shops lining the street, the sounds of Christmas carols floated through the air. I tucked my head under the hood of my coat to block out the sights and sounds around me. They only made me more homesick.

Light flurries of snow swirled against me as I quickened my pace. I'd soon be home. Crossing the street, I saw the

big church on the corner. It was aglow with lots of candles burning brightly inside. A life-size crèche stood on the lawn with Joseph and Mary looking down at the Christ Child in the manger. A lighted sign next to it read: "Please join us for Midnight Mass on Christmas Eve." A tear slipped down my cheek. Midnight Mass was a tradition our family never missed. We *always* went to church *together* on Christmas Eve. To go without them would only add to the pain I already felt in being alone. *Why,* I thought, *do I have to be 6,000 miles from home this night?*

Inside the entrance way to my building I fumbled for my keys. Then I heard it. A soft, vaguely familiar voice singing: "Joy to the world, the Lord is come . . ." I stopped and looked around. No one was there. I listened curiously. "Let earth receive her King . . ." I poked my head into the street. No one. I looked at the intercom unit on my right, and then I understood. The voice was coming from its speaker. Of course! It belonged to Mrs. Julia on the sixth floor. Mrs. Julia was a widow who lived alone in 6-B. She was a hearty soul who loved to stop residents in the lobby to chat—endlessly. More than once she'd told me more than I wanted to know about her herb garden and Felix, her house cat. Though she was a kind woman—she brought me chicken soup one afternoon when she heard I had the flu—I had been avoiding her recently. I knew she was lonely, but I just didn't have the time to listen to her nonstop chatter. Now, I could picture her sitting on the wooden stool next to the voice box in her kitchen, her wiry, silver hair tousled into a bun atop her head, singing to her neighbors as they came home.

As I listened my body lightened. Her voice rang out . . . "Let ev'ry heart . . . prepare Him room . . ." The words awakened me like a splash of cold water on my face. *"Prepare Him room"* . . . *Why, this is what Christmas is about,* I thought, *preparing room for Christ in my heart.* My mind raced back over the last few weeks. Had I prepared Him room? No, I hadn't. I had been too busy missing my family and friends. And in my loneliness I had *closed* my heart as tight as a clenched fist. To really celebrate Christmas meant I would have to *open* my heart—then I could make room for others. Maybe Christmas wouldn't have to be lonely after all.

Leaning against the intercom box, I drank in Mrs. Julia's radiant voice. "We wish you a Merry Christmas . . . we wish you a Merry Christmas . . ." she sang loudly. I pressed my finger on the button next to 6-B.

"Mrs. Julia," I said. "Mrs. Julia, this is Terri Castillo—down in 2-C."

"Merry Christmas, Terri!" she chimed back to me.

"Mrs. Julia," I said as a smile crossed my face, "how would you like to go to Midnight Mass with me tonight?"*

*Reprinted with permission from *The Guideposts Family Christmas Book.* Copyright © 1980 by Guideposts Associates, Inc., Carmel, NY 10512.

SEVEN

The Christmas Survey

How to create the holiday
you really want

Here is a chance to focus on your own private Christmas expectations and wishes and to compare your idea of a "dream" Christmas with what *really* happens at your house. Taking this short test will help determine whether or not you are expecting too much from the holidays and if you are using limited time and energy to get what you really want. The results will help set priorities and give an emphatic no to less important things. You will find ways to set aside time for really meaningful activities, and you will discover more peace of mind. You will feel better steering your celebration in the direction you choose, even if the change takes several years to accomplish.

Go through the survey with *red* pencil and check in the left-hand column the six items that have top priority and are absolute "firsts" in importance to you. Now check the next six most important with *blue* pencil. The others items obviously rate lower and become optional. In the boxes at the right, check those things you actually experienced last Christmas. Comparing right- and left-hand columns will help you gain a clearer picture of where you need to make changes. This will help you make the holidays come alive, until they are closer to what you had in mind all along. Maybe you can get your spouse and the kids to take the Christmas survey, too.

I Want

I Experienced:

_____ To have my family all together over the holidays _____

Who?_____

How? _____

_____ To spend lots of time at home in family fun activities _____

GREAT CHRISTMAS IDEAS

	I Want	**I Experienced:**

I Want

I Experienced:

_____ To make our family's home activities closely match the real meaning of Christmas.   _____

How? _____

_____ To emphasize the religious part of Christmas in church   _____

How? _____

Which church?_____

_____ To be sure my holiday values are shared with the children   _____

How? _____

Which values? _____

_____ To play down Santa to the children   _____

How? _____

_____ To have enough money to buy gifts I feel are necessary   _____

How? _____

_____ To spend less money   _____

_____ To be creative in making and giving gifts that cost less or nothing at all   _____

_____ To express my love clearly to family and friends in ways other than giving gifts   _____

How? _____

_____ To get Christmas shopping done ahead   _____

How? _____

When?_____

		I Experienced:
I Want		

_____ To slow down and avoid December pressure by _____
doing other activities ahead

Which ones?_____

When?_____

_____ To go shopping at a special mall or take a trip _____
to a big city department store

_____ To entertain in my home _____

Who?_____

How?_____

_____ To simplify Christmas, to have less rushing _____
around

How?_____

_____ To experience the peace of Christmas _____

How?_____

_____ To enjoy the music, the spirit, the excitement and _____
beauty of the season, special foods, new people

How?_____

_____ To visit special friends or relatives who live far _____
away

Who?_____

_____ To attend parties given by others _____

Important ones: _____

_____ To do more for others, to give more of my time _____
and talent

How?_____

GREAT CHRISTMAS IDEAS

I Want		I Experienced:
_____	To give money or gifts to individuals in need or to charities	_____
	Which? _____	
	How much?_____	
_____	To pay personal visits to a few favorite people nearby	_____
	Who?_____	
	How? _____	
_____	To make up with someone I have hurt	_____
	Who?_____	
	How? _____	
_____	To celebrate our family's traditions	_____
	Which ones?_____	
_____	To break off old traditions and make new ones	_____
	Break off which ones?_____	
	Make which new ones?_____	
_____	To travel and get away for solitude during the holidays	_____
_____	To send out Christmas cards	_____
_____	To receive special gifts I have been wanting	_____
_____	To plan a Christmas party at work	_____
_____	To be sure I have a clean house	_____
_____	To do a great job of decorating my house	_____
_____	To do ____ more ____ less baking	_____
_____	To get through December without gaining weight	_____
	How? _____	
_____	To have snow	_____

I Want		I Experienced:
_____	To be able to accept our family as they are, without harping or argument	_____
	Other things I want from Christmas:	
_____	1. _____	_____
_____	2. _____	_____
_____	3. _____	_____
_____	4. _____	_____

Above all, do your best to keep your expectations realistic. Perhaps your heart's desire can never be realized. If your daughter has experienced a divorce and the court has awarded Christmas visiting rights for your grandson to her ex-husband, then stop yearning for "perfect family" closeness. Instead, consider establishing off-season celebrations. If you know that cranky Uncle Ralph will be spending Christmas Day with family as usual, and that your Mom's arthritis is growing more painful . . . and neither situation is likely to change, then revise your expectations. Concentrate on resetting your priorities and making the necessary changes to fit those true, realistic priorities.

Decide what fits your schedule, your budget, your situation. Maybe family and children's activities come before "adults only" parties, or perhaps making sure the holiday table has the finest of everything is not as important as time spent visiting elderly parents. Which is more important: making certain that Great-grandmother's traditional plum pudding gets served, or that the family attends Midnight Mass? Maybe you are a single mother and you lack the energy and the money to go to where your clan gathers every Christmas. You are probably the only one who truly real-

izes the difficulty of coping with a baby or squabbling preschoolers for five or six hours in the car. Why not visit your hometown in the summer instead, when you can talk a friend with vacation time into going along to help out with the children? Take the pressure off of yourself by refusing to hold to tradition when it can't realistically be done.

Use this Christmas survey to sort through your traditions, then decide what you really want to do—and go for it! Traditions that are chosen, not imposed, make strong positive family ties.

EIGHT

Safe Holiday Checklist

Seasonal reminders to make sure
everyone enjoys the season safely

Christmas, with all its merry-making, brings a special set of hazards. With the house all aglow and filled with people, holiday celebrations can easily be dampened by mishaps. We are more apt to become careless about safety details because there is so much to think about, and so many exciting events are brewing. Still, it pays to take the time to ensure your holiday will be as safe as possible.

Use this checklist to have a safer, more enjoyable holiday season.

- Make sure the tree you choose is freshly cut. Take it down when needles begin to dry out. Studies show that it takes just twenty-seven seconds for an eight-foot tree to burn. Spray-on products added to the water may add to the life of the tree, but make little difference in flammability.

- Place the tree in an area where connections will not get bumped. Make sure the stand is big enough so it will not topple over.

- If you use an artificial tree, check label or box for instructions. Some trees have a limit on the number of years that fireproofing is sustained.

- Electric lights should never, never be used on an aluminum tree. If lights short out, somebody coming by to touch the tree could be shocked or even electrocuted. Instead, use colored spotlights set above or beside the tree.

- Keep a fire extinguisher handy, making sure it can be used for electrical fires (there are different kinds for different kinds of fires), and be certain that everybody in the family

237

knows how to use it. In case of emergency, begin spraying, using a side to side motion, about six to eight feet away. Slowly work your way toward the fire with the nozzle aimed at the base of the flames. The room needs to be ventilated afterward. Never use water on electrical fires.

- Check light strings for fraying and exposed wires. Discard those with loose connections or broken sockets. One single exposed strand can cause a shock or a fire. Rubber or plastic cords that lay around in attics or closet boxes often harden and crack. Date electric lights and extension cords so you know when it is time to replace them.

- Look for sturdy wires when buying electric decorations. Small wires break more easily. Use care in handling lights, especially miniature sets, which are more fragile. Be sure to purchase extra bulbs when buying light strings so they fit perfectly when needed later. Purchase only UL-certified replacement light sets, extension cords, and decorations (such as lighted Santas). Never connect miniature sets to traditional ones, nor floodlights to regular Christmas light strings of any kind.

- Be careful not to overload electrical outlets. Never use a plug or cord that becomes hot or very warm to the touch during use. Keep lighted bulbs well away from flammable decorations, such as those made of cardboard or paper.

- Position the off-on switch away from the tree for easy access in case of fire. Keep distance between electrical connections and the tree's water supply. Turn tree and wreath lights off at

bedtime and before leaving home, even if there is a baby-sitter in the house. She may not be as safety-minded as you are.

- If light set instructions say "For indoor use only," do not display them outside. They are not waterproof and could short out, which could cause a fire, if it rains or snows. Similarly, lights marked for outdoors will probably generate too much heat to be used safely inside. Check the label to be certain all outdoor lights are weatherproof. Check extension cords, too!

- Keep extension cords short and out of traffic areas. It is not a good idea to coil the cords since coiling dissipates heat unevenly, drying out the cord in places to make it a potential fire hazard. Never run a cord under a rug or drape it over a surface like a stove, furnace pipe, or radiator that may get hot later.

- Keep electric toys, like train and racing car sets, and small appliances that may spark away from the tree. (Have a question about an electric toy or gadget received for Christmas? Call the Consumer Product Safety Commission hotline at 1-800-638-CPSC.)

- Be especially watchful of babies and cats, who will sometimes chew on extension cords. And keep an eye out for toddlers, who may stick hairpins or other metal objects into electric plugs, resulting in burns or shock.

- Keep lighted candles on higher tables or shelves, out of the reach of young children. Use extreme care when combining candles and cut greens for use as table centerpieces or other displays. Use flameproof holders and keep candles

away from crowded areas where they can get knocked over. Blow them out unless someone is there to keep a constant watch.

- Avoid tree trimmings that look edible. Small children or pets can choke on tinsel, little pieces of ribbon, tiny ornaments, or little parts from toy sets. Sweep up dry needles. Artificial snow rubbed in the eyes, swallowed, or inhaled can cause serious damage, too. Bubbling tree lights contain a chemical which can be dangerous if bulbs are swallowed. Children should not be allowed to handle angel hair decorations. Adults should wear gloves when handling these ornaments since angel hair is made from fiberglass, which can penetrate skin and get in eyes. Consider giving kids their own tree to decorate with harmless paper chains, candy canes, and cookies.

- Remember that mistletoe, holly, and poinsettia foliage can be poisonous if ingested by children or pets. Other plants considered hazardous are amaryllis, azalea, Christmas cactus, Christmas rose, crown of thorns, English or American ivy, Jerusalem or Christmas cherry, balsam fir, privet, and rhododendron.

- Keep half-filled glasses of alcohol out of the reach of children. Be especially alert at parties.

- Never dispose of Christmas wrapping in a woodstove or fireplace. Much of the ink used in making colored paper contains lead, which can end up polluting the air or building up inside the chimney.

Safety for Houseguests

■ Help prevent falls by shovelling slippery snow and ice off of steps, driveways, and walkways or by throwing on calcium chloride pellets.

■ Never wax floors so that they are super-slick just before a party. Store small throw rugs that may trip unwary or elderly guests.

■ Keep stairways and hallways unobstructed. Ask children to do an especially good job picking up toys, particularly if visitors are older folks.

■ Plug night lights in guest bedrooms or areas where people are likely to walk on their way to the bathroom at night. Guests can easily stumble and fall trying to find their way in an unfamiliar house.

■ Let guests know about any emergency fire escape plan that you and your family have rehearsed. This is especially important if you have an overflow holiday crowd sleeping on floors or in the attic spaces and cellar rooms.

■ Make sure that smoke alarms are in perfect working order. Some have tester buttons for checking batteries, or you can hold a candle under each to listen for buzzer reaction. It may be a good idea simply to write a reminder on the calendar to replace all smoke detector batteries each year on December 1.

■ Many holiday recipes call for cooking with wines and liquors. Because alcohol is a form of fuel, it can cause an unexpected flash fire if improperly used. Follow recipe amounts exactly since using too much alcohol in a small, hot

space like an oven can ignite it. Some home economists recommend that dishes containing alcohol be cooked uncovered to prevent heat from building up under the cover—perhaps even causing an explosion. Generally speaking, cook these spirited dishes by themselves, if possible. The larger the oven, the safer you are.

Epilogue

I hope by now that your mind is overflowing with bright new ideas about Christmas and that you are enthusiastic about making some of these ideas actually happen in your home. If only a few of us escape the "ghosts of Christmas past" and learn to celebrate the Yule season more creatively (not compulsively!) and with more purpose, then perhaps our children, too, will begin to discover more joy and meaning in this wonderful season. And perhaps they will begin to establish their own creative traditions and one day pass them on to yet another generation.

May you and yours be able to find the *real* Christmas and learn to celebrate it in ways that honor our Lord.